# POSITIVE NETWORKING

## How to network effectively – and how not to!

To Bev
Best wishes
[illegible]
6/2/24

# CONTENTS

**Introduction**

**Part 1 Finding & Evaluating Networking Groups**

**Part 2 Effective Networking (How To Do It)**

**Part 3 Ineffective Networking (How Not To Do It)**

**Part 4 Building, Growing and Maintaining a Networking Club**

**Part 5 Presentations On The Subject Of Networking**
a) Destroying The Myths Of Networking
b) Effective Online Networking
c) Five Ps Of Networking
d) Hey, It's Networking Not Selling
e) Is Your Networking NOT Working?
f) Networking Encyclopaedia
g) Networking Jungle
h) Ten Commandments Of Networking
i) Three Biggest Mistakes Of Networking
j) Working The Room

**Part 6 Ice-breakers**
Birthday Line
Listen 1 and Listen 2
Present And Back
Revealing Threesomes
So What?
Thanks For The Memory

**Part 7 Making Rounds Of Elevator Pitches More Interesting**
a) Seasonal Themes

b) Current Themes
c) Historical Themes
d) Procedural Variations

Part 8 Twenty Different Networking Formats
(i) Acid Test
(ii) Ask Our Geeks
(iii) Boundarylessness
(iv) Bring A Prop
(v) Deck Of Cards
(vi) Flipchart Fiesta
(vii) Getting To Know You
(viii) Hammering Out A Deal
(ix) Knowledge Carousel
(x) Matrix Networking
(xi) Mini Boardroom
(xii) Monopoly Of Wisdom
(xiii) Networking Bingo
(xiv) Networking Safari
(xv) Open And Closed
(xvi) Pair And Share
(xvii) Send Three And Fourpence
(xviii) Spanish Inquisition
(xix) Speaker Event
(xx) Speed Networking

Part 9 Closing Advice

# INTRODUCTION

"The secret of business is knowing something that nobody else knows." (Aristotle Onassis)

"Business has only two functions – marketing and innovation." (Peter Drucker)

Back in the early 1970s, as a young Commercial Apprentice, I remember looking at the Managing Director of the company where I was employed. I decided then, that for me to get on and climb up the slippery corporate ladder, I would need to regularly advertise myself and my attributes to the people between myself and the Managing Director. Over the next 33 years I did just that – taking every opportunity to let the senior managers and directors know who I was and what I could do. As a result, I was promoted twelve times within the organisation, ending up as Export Director - but I only ever applied for one of those positions. In every other case, I was offered a job because they knew exactly what they were getting. Without realising it, I had been networking.

At the end of 2003 I left corporate life and started up as a freelance export adviser, confident in my knowledge of international trade, comforted by having two ready-made clients, but not really knowing how prospective clients were going to find me. Yes, I had a few target organisations in mind – but no definite plan for spreading the word amongst unknown prospects. When the fledgling business was 6 weeks old, my wife saw an article in the local paper about a club for local businesses which helped its members to meet, share experiences and find new customers. So I went along to The Business Club in Peterborough for my first formal experience of business networking.

I remember my first experiences there, and I tried hard to replicate them later on when I was "on the other side". Upon arrival, I was told how pleased the organisers were to meet me, they outlined the programme for the evening, introduced me to two existing members and led me to the food. The first half of the meeting consisted of (about 60) elevator pitches and the second half included Chris Billington-Hughes, a very inspiring speaker. I left with lots of ideas for my new business and a number of new contacts.

My experience at my second meeting was very similar – but then I started wondering how I would get any business from my new-found contacts, as none of them seemed likely to need my niche services. The answer came on the morning after my third networking meeting. An accountant called me, as he had seen me at the previous evening's meeting. He had a client who was looking to export, but didn't know how or where to start. He wondered if that was the kind of thing I did.

Now I understood how this networking thing worked. It was about building relationships, earning respect and building trust. And then people told other people about you. **It was selling THROUGH people and not selling TO people**. It took me three meetings to understand this most important principle of networking – and I have spent some years since then helping others to recognise it.

Having seen how my business could prosper by using The Business Club, I proceeded to try as many different networking groups as I could within 50 miles of Peterborough. I learned how to promote my business, how to develop business relationships and how to be a better business owner by attending meetings run by Huntingdonshire Business Network, The Missing Link, Lincoln Business Club, Newark Business Club, Total Networking (Grantham), Spalding Business Club, Lincoln Enterprise Network, Cambridgeshire Chamber of

Commerce and Lincolnshire Chamber of Commerce. I also tried a number of BNI meetings but, although I absolutely got why BNI was so successful, it just didn't seem right for me. My general networking experience stood me in good stead when attending export-specific events and it is true to say that by 2009 almost all of my business had come directly or indirectly through networking.

I was able to see that networkers got different things from different groups, I could see how other networkers worked the room more than others and I could see how inexperienced business owners could use other networkers as sounding boards or mentors. I recognised how networking events could be far more than just rounds of elevator pitches.

The Business Club had been founded in the mid 1990s by Brian Soanes and Lesley Lambert. When Brian approached me in 2009 about starting up a franchise in Lincolnshire, I just had to be interested. I liked the format, the values and the results of The Business Club so I took on my new role as a franchisee with relish. After three years, the franchise arrangement ceased but my wife and I carried on the Lincoln club as our own independent business, still using some of Brian's formats but also introducing many of our own. For a year, we dabbled with a version of the club just for new businesses (New2Business) and we also ran The Business Club for six months in Grantham.

At the end of 2015 we merged the club with Sukhi Wahiwala's Peterborough-based Inspired Business Club to form Positive Networking. We operated in Lincoln and

Peterborough, offering the greatest range of networking formats anywhere. Details of those formats (twenty of them) are covered in the second half of this book. When the Covid lockdown arrived, we started running virtual networking meetings but we recognised that after the lockdown it would take a lot of time and effort to re-build Positive Networking back to where it had been, so we called it a day in June 2020.

Over the years I have seen why networking worked, and why it did not. I have experienced and invented some very effective networking formats and learned how to apply them. This book seeks to teach business networkers how to get the most out of their networking. It also gives business network organisers plenty of ideas on how to keep things fresh, how to ensure networkers enjoy themselves and how to give networkers real takeaways for their businesses.

You will see throughout the book that, whilst I advocate variety and a certain amount of fun in networking events, it must not be forgotten that networking is a serious business activity and forms an important element within a business' marketing strategy.

# PART 1

# FINDING & EVALUATING NETWORKING GROUPS

"Advice is what we ask for when we already know the answer but we wish that we didn't." (Erica Jong)

"Creative people must entertain lots of silly ideas in order to receive the occasional strokes of genius." (Marshall Cook)

Finding networking groups which are appropriate for your business is really important, as is the evaluation of those groups. Networking activities can be a very important part of a business' marketing strategy, so it is vital that the right groups are identified and it is just as important that the success or otherwise of those groups is reviewed and measured. So, how do you find networking groups which are "right" for you?

***Objectives*** – before embarking upon any networking activity, consider first what you want to get out of it. Most people say they are doing it so that they can increase the value of their sales, and very understandable that is. But I always contend that what they really want to do is to grow their bottom line profits. So, it is not just potential customers they are seeking, they are also looking for people who have existing relationships with such potential customers. Every potential customer has dealings with printers, accountants, web designers etc, so finding that kind of organisation can get you in front of customers in an indirect way. Finding alternative suppliers, advisers and experts can take cost out of your business and leave you with a healthier bottom line. One of the members of the club I ran often told me that he got no extra sales from his networking – but he reduced his annual costs by £26000 as a result of the alternative suppliers he met (printers, builders, cleaners, web designers etc).
So, the first consideration is "why am I doing this?"

***Profile Of Attendee*** – having established why you want to go networking, you now need to recognise which networking groups attract the kind of businesses you would like to meet. Sometimes you can get a fair idea from the groups' websites, from social media activity,

from other networkers or from press articles. But the best way is to go along, attend a meeting and find out for yourself.
I once attended a meeting of the Cambridge High Tech Association of Small Enterprises (CHASE) as it had been recommended to me. Once inside, it soon became apparent that I was easily the thickest person in the room. The other attendees had gone along, not for general business networking, but to chat with similar individuals about technology and its development. The room was full of eggheads … and one village idiot!
You need to establish the type of people who attend each group – sole traders, manufacturers, professionals, creative industries, business service providers etc. And it is a two-way exercise – so how could you help them?
Once you have attended a meeting, ask the other attendees to recommend other groups. Many groups will let you attend one meeting free of charge – but don't expect this.

***Frequency Of Meetings*** – you need to find out how often various groups meet – weekly, fortnightly, monthly. How much of a commitment will this be and how will it fit in with the rest of your personal and business activities?

***Timing Of Meetings*** – this can be critical as networking activity has to fit in with the rest of your business life, your family life and your social life. Some groups meet early in the morning (before the business day starts), others meet during the day (often at lunchtime) and others meet in the evening (after the business day finishes). It often makes sense to build a package of networking groups, meeting at different times of the day, to enable you to pick up different types of business.

***Style Of Meetings*** – every group will have its own framework, wrapped around teas and coffees, buffet food or a more formal "sit down" meal. Some groups will include a round of 60 seconds "elevator pitches", others will include table-swapping, one-to-one sessions and exchanges of referrals. Often, groups will use external guest speakers to educate, stimulate and entertain the attendees. Others will use a variety of participative activities, such as those covered later in this book. Some networking groups will "grow on you" but by and large you normally know early on if a group feels comfortable for you.

***Geography*** – the location of meetings is important, especially if the group meets very early or very late. It also needs to be considered from what sort of area each group draws in its participants. A group, which meets a number of miles away might just provide a gateway to lots of previously unreachable contacts. However, you need to be sure you can adequately cover the area in which your fellow networkers are located. The availability of online meetings has added another factor as business people seek to put together a "package" of networking events for themselves.

***Cost*** – some online groups are free of charge, some face-to-face groups may charge on the door, others only take advance payments, and some may charge on an annual basis. It is not possible (because of cost and time) to attend every single networking meeting. Networkers therefore have to compare the cost of each group with what they are looking to get out of the relationship.

***Membership Structure*** – some groups just charge for attendance and do not use a formal membership structure. Others insist upon a membership, which might include sector exclusivity, inclusion on the group's website, access to training, the right to give presentations at meetings and access to group discounts. Potential members should consider how long they must commit before putting pen to paper.

Having established which groups are likely to be the best for your business, how do you measure your performance at these groups?

***Sales leads*** – measure the leads you get and not the value of the resultant sales. The job of the networking group is to put you in front of useful people, the conversion rate is your responsibility. Having said that, it may be possible to meet fellow networkers with expertise in lead conversion and sales closure.

***Contact with intermediaries*** – people who know your potential customers are very valuable (business coaches, specialist advisers, IT providers etc) so it is important to record how many contacts you pick up from your networking meetings.

***New supplier introductions*** – remember that the bottom line of your business is more important than your top line. The networking circuit can put you in front of experts who can help you to reduce the costs in your business – people like SEO specialists, telecoms experts, energy brokers etc. By asking for help, these experts can help you to improve your profits – and then other experts can help you to pay less tax.

***Collaboration opportunities*** – sometimes you can develop your business by working alongside another business. This could be someone who does not supply the same product but they deal with the same potential customers.

***Self or staff development*** – your own business expertise can be enhanced by regular contact with other businesses, learning of others' experiences and sharing of problems. External experts can be used as guest speakers, challenging and educating the attendees. The effect of networking could well be a more-rounded team.

***Cost-effectiveness*** – at the end of the day the question has to be asked "am I getting good value?" By looking closely at the items above and comparing those items with the annual cost of networking with a group, it can be decided if there are areas for concern. No-one has the time or the money to belong to every networking group, so it is important to develop the right cluster of groups. Networkers must go back to their initial objectives – why they decided to go networking in the first place. They must then compare those objectives with the outcomes measured above. If a group is not working for you, it is necessary to meet with that group's organiser to understand whether (a) it is your fault, (b) you have been unlucky or (c) the group is just not the right one for you. Networkers should constantly review the groups they use and the value they are getting from each.

# PART 2

# EFFECTIVE NETWORKING

"People don't want to be MARKETED TO, they want to be COMMUNICATED WITH." (Flint McGlaughlin)

"There is one way to find out if a man is honest – ask him. If he says Yes, you know he is crooked." (Groucho Marx)

Business networking has often been dismissed as being a bunch of casual business folks getting together with their pals for coffee and cakes. And, if you don't organise yourself, that is all it might be. But most people go into the networking world in order to grow their businesses and they have to discipline themselves to ensure that they get the desired results. I have contended for years that the route towards effective networking can be illustrated via ***The Five Ps Of Networking – Preparation, Performance, Pitch, Patience and Persistence.***

***PREPARATION***

Every time that you attend a business meeting with your staff, suppliers, bank or customers, you will prepare yourself for the meeting to ensure that you achieve your objectives and present your points comprehensively. Going to networking events (where you may meet potential customers or suppliers) should call for the same degree of professionalism. You need to come across as knowledgeable, polished and approachable.
This may sound very basic but understanding the ***actual location*** of the meeting is important. Do you know the site, the building and the room number? Can you park there? How far is it from a car park, railway station, bus stop etc? How much time should you allow yourself to travel there? When you walk into the room, that will be the first time some people will have seen you. Think how unimpressive it will be if you get there 15 minutes after everyone else, looking disorganised and dishevelled. Think what that says about your business – will people think that you will fail to deliver your product or service on time?

If you are attending a new group for the first time, contact the organisers to establish the ***exact timing***. Does the published time include pre-meeting mingling or is that the time the meeting starts? Remember that being punctual creates a very positive impression of your business, so get the time right.
Make sure that you know what ***format*** the meeting will follow, especially recognising the time allotted for you to pitch your business. Find out beforehand if you are allowed to take leaflets, samples, display banners etc. If there are to be round table discussions, you may wish to prepare some notes.
Try to find out who else will be at the meeting and consider the ***dress code***. My advice is to turn up in a way in which prospective customers would expect to see you. If you are a chartered accountant or lawyer, it wouldn't make sense for you to present yourself looking like a refugee from Glastonbury! Casual clothing works fine as long as it is smart and clean. And, as you are keen to creative a positive first impression on new business contacts, treat it as seriously as you would on a first date – clean hair, trimmed nails, sweet breath, suitable make-up, polished shoes and so on.
Not many networking events are free of charge, so find out beforehand what the ***cost*** is and how you can pay. Some groups will require a hefty annual subscription and it makes sense to get an idea of this before attending meetings. Other groups will just require you to pay for individual meetings. Find out whether the quoted costs include food and drink, otherwise you may get a surprise.
It will help if you can get an idea from the organisers who the ***attendees*** will be – how many will there be and what kind of businesses will be there? You will need to tailor your pitch, depending on whether you are talking to micro

business owners, large company directors, charities, tradesmen, service providers and consultants. See if you can get a list of attendees before the meeting, so you can look out for certain interesting individuals.

For you to measure whether your networking is effective or not, you need to be clear what your ***objectives*** are. If you can't clarify why you are attending, you can't determine whether or not you have achieved a good result. Give yourself some key takeaways – number of new contacts, number of one-to-one follow up meetings arranged, new ideas to try immediately, names of new suppliers etc. Longer term, you should log the new business you receive through each networking group, to see which ones work.

Don't forget the "Must Take" items which you should always have with you when attending networking events:-

***Business cards*** – prior to the Covid crisis, these were the most fundamental tools in a networker's toolbox. Although some networkers now prefer to receive digital business cards, you just might need one physical card for every attendee, so make sure you take enough. Your cards should be legible (try to avoid white or grey on a black background) and not cheap-looking.

If you decide to use people's business cards to build up a database of contacts, make sure that you comply with Data Protection guidelines, asking for permission where appropriate.

***Pen and notebook*** – you will learn things about people and you may pick up some sound takeaways from speakers, so make sure you can capture that data. Of course, you can also capture such data on your tablet.

***Diary*** – if you meet someone interesting and decide to meet up for a one-to-one meeting, strike while the iron is

hot. Get a date in your diary straight away, it is far more difficult to obtain dates in the days after the meeting.
***Flyers and leaflets*** – check first with the organisers, but it is usually possible to take literature with you. Try to stick to A4 folded in 3 as this size is easy for jacket pockets and handbags. Any handout which is unwieldy will invariably still be lying on the table after the event has finished.
***Badge*** – if the organisers do not provide badges, invest in your own badge, complete with logo and a clear name. Those with magnetic backs are the best, as they do not damage your clothing, and they can be used with just about every outfit. It makes good sense to keep a spare badge in your car, just in case.
***Notes*** – if you manage to obtain a speaker slot, you will need supporting notes. Also, if you feel more comfortable keeping a "crib sheet" for your elevator pitch, then don't be afraid to do so.
***"Non-Selling" Mindset*** – one of the biggest mistakes made by networkers is in confusing networking with selling. Networking is all about building relationships and creating reputations for you and your business. Pinning people against the wall and selling at them is quite the wrong approach to take. Remember to ask for help rather than for an order. Try to see every other delegate, not as a potential target, but as someone who has lots of new and useful contacts for you.

## *PERFORMANCE*

Having established your objectives, it is important that you make things happen if your networking is to be fully effective. You cannot just turn up and hope that opportunities will drop in your lap, it is important that you are proactive.

Try to ***be one of the first delegates to arrive***, as the best quality networking often takes place while the room is gradually filling up. Being punctual is a great first impression to make and you have more time to meet new people to start building relationships. And of course, you just might get to pick a decent seat for yourself to catch any speaker presentations.

One good networker I knew always positioned himself by the tea and coffee, offering to pour drinks for other delegates. This sounds corny, but immediately he established himself as a nice, helpful and friendly face with the other networkers.

If you arrive at a networking event with one of your ***colleagues***, leave them after you have checked in. You already know them, so don't waste your time by chatting and sipping coffee with them – you need to ***"work the room".***

- There will be "singletons" standing all on their own, probably not having attended the group before. This is a chance to create a really good first impression, put them at their ease and introduce them to others.
- "Closed twos" are standing pretty much face-to-face and their body language suggests they do not want to be interrupted – so don't! People who are having serious business discussions with customers or suppliers will not be happy with rude interruptions, so respect such scenarios and catch them later.
- "Open twos" have a more open stance (not face-to-face) and quite clearly can be approached, especially if you already know one of them. Just

push yourself in and ask the person you know to introduce you to the other.
- Similarly, groups of three or more will nearly always have an "open corner" into which you can slip.
- Apart from the "closed twos", no-one else will object to your approach because networking is exactly what they have gone along to do!

***Here are "7 Killer Questions"*** to glean information about people, making use of open questions throughout:-
- What does your business do?
- When did you start doing this?
- Where are you based?
- Why are your products or services different?
- Who are your customers?
- Which methods do you use to find new customers?
- How can I help you?

***Do not stay with the same people too long***, you need to move on. If you are struggling to get away from another networker, you can make out that you need a coffee, or that you need the toilet. But I find the most effective way is to introduce them to someone you know – and then clear off! It is vital that you make the most of the allotted time for open networking so, although it may seem harsh to pass people on, these things have to be done.
Keep yourself ***cool and hydrated***. Of course, the coffee is very pleasant – but water is better for you, especially as you will be talking a lot. I recommend that you avoid alcohol until after your networking meeting has finished.
Try to establish yourself as a ***connector of people***, so introduce others and get yourself introduced. Ask questions of other delegates and show an interest in their

replies. Make connections and do not sell. Spend twice as much time listening as you do talking.
Even if you are not quizzing anyone, be a ***good listener*** at networking events. Listen out for the topics people are discussing, listen to the way other networkers present themselves and, above all, listen out for what people need. If you can be seen to be helping other networkers that creates a really positive image for you and your business, especially as the helped person will tell others about you.
***Collect business cards*** and write on the back of each card what action you are going to take (call, email, invite, pass on etc). After meeting a lot of people, it can be difficult to remember what action you ought to take several days after the event if you haven't written it down. However, if a person is from the Far East, you must NOT write on their business card as it would be deemed to be insulting. The practice there is to scrutinise and respect business cards and not to scribble on them.
We saw how good quality networking can be experienced before a meeting starts, and the same is true after the official end of the meeting. Try to ***linger at the end*** and catch those people you may have missed earlier. Before leaving, try to give yourself just five minutes to write down your actions – who will you call, who will you email, who will you send social media connection requests to, what takeaways do you have from the speaker?

### *PITCH*

At every networking event you will ever attend, there will be an opportunity to make a "pitch" – on a one-to-one basis, to a table of other delegates or maybe to the whole room. Delivering an effective and memorable pitch is fundamentally important if your networking is to work, so

spend lots of time preparing it, writing it and rehearsing it. Don't just wing it!
As part of your preparation for the event, you will have established what the ***format of the meeting*** is and you will know how long you will get to make a pitch. There may be an opportunity for informal face-to-face networking before the main event, in which case you will need to keep a 30 seconds introductory pitch up your sleeve, and then you will get a chance to formally pitch to a bigger group later. Most groups give you 60 seconds but some of the larger gatherings only allow you 45 or even 30 seconds, so you must prepare for every eventuality. I have normally prepared a 60 seconds pitch and then, if allotted more than that, I have thrown in a couple of examples of the type of clients I have worked with.
There is often a bright spark at an event who ignores the imposed time limit and carries on pitching, as though their message is more important than everyone else's. This just irritates the other attendees, so don't be that person!
It is important that you ***structure your pitch and then rehearse it*** until you have (a) included everything you need and (b) finished just inside the allotted time. In practice, in front of a large gathering, most of us deliver our pitches slightly more quickly than during our rehearsals. Don't forget to draw breath!
There have been books and articles written about how to deliver a memorable pitch. The model I like best was given to me by a very inspiring speaker from Newark, Keith Warren. Keith ran practical exercises to prove that people remember things mentioned at the beginning of a presentation far better than the things they hear towards the end. He also stressed that delegates don't really care about your pitch – they are just listening for "what's in it for them?" Taking those two things together, you should

tell people what they want to hear at the beginning of your pitch and not towards the end. ***This is the structure I recommend*** for your elevator pitch: -

- Try to avoid starting your pitch while you are still scraping your chair across the floor
- Stand still, take a deep breath and avoid speaking too quickly
- After gathering yourself, clearly state your name and the name of your business
- Stress the benefits or results of your product or service
- Explain, clearly and without jargon, how you deliver those results
- Include something visual (an object, an action or even a hand gesture)
- Give examples of the types of customers you serve
- Make it clear what help you are seeking
- Let the recipients feel that they are being informed, not sold to
- Finish by stating again your name and your business

Or, putting it simply: -

*This is who I am*
*This is the benefit of what I do*
*This is how I do it*
*This is who I do it for*
*This is what I need*
*And this is who I am again*

Some people like to use "crib notes" and if this makes you more comfortable then use them, but try to avoid just standing up and blatantly reading out your pitch. If you are able to use comedy to good effect, then use it – but it can

be very cringeworthy if this is not your forte. If you inject comedy, make sure you do not trivialise your product or service. Try to avoid abbreviations, buzz words and cliches which are only understood within your niche or sector. And don't be afraid to ask other networkers about your pitch – do they now understand what you are offering?
This is your shop window, an opportunity to demonstrate how professional, knowledgeable and approachable you are. Be clear, be concise and (above all else) ***be memorable***.

***PATIENCE***

Because networking is all about relationship-building, and not about instant selling, it cannot be regarded as a "quick fix". You will often hear people say that they tried a group twice but didn't get any leads, so they are not going to attend again. Research has shown that it takes 4 to 7 contacts before someone recommends you and, if you think about it, that's probably about right. If you recommend someone, you are risking your own reputation as well as that of the person you are recommending. You are only going to refer someone when you are sure that they will not let you down – and ***it will take a few contacts*** before you reach that stage.
When you join a new group, you must give it chance to work. You need to give the other delegates time to understand what it is you are offering and therefore what help you are seeking. Regularly check with some of the other delegates if they understand your offering – and, if not, review your pitch. Look at the type of businesses in the group and whether you are making it clear how you can help them.

It is important that you maintain regular, polite contact with the people you have met, without expecting a quick return. Remind other networkers what you are looking for, without becoming a nuisance. Be seen to be making referrals for other members of the group. Over a period of time, you will generally ***get back what you have put in***.

## *PERSISTENCE*

It is not enough just to turn up at networking events and tell people what you do. That is only the start of a lengthy process which requires organisation and dedication. Failing to follow up is one of the most common reasons why networking is ineffective for people. Here then is a step-by-step guide on ***how to follow-up***: -

- At the end of a networking meeting, do not charge off into the car park. Instead, before leaving the meeting venue, just sit down for five minutes and ***compile a list of actions*** which you will take forward. This could include people to call, people to email, invitations to send, referrals to make, takeaways from the speaker and the arranging of one-to-one meetings.
- ***Get in touch*** with other networkers without delay, certainly within 48 hours, while you are still fresh in their minds. Maybe you should avoid contacting people as soon as you get back to your base, as it may just smack of desperation! Connecting via social media makes good sense as you start to forge these new relationships but take care not to bombard folks with too many requests.
- Whatever you have promised to do, make sure you do so ***swiftly*** (sending emails, making referrals

etc). This will create a very positive image for you and your business.

- Don't just follow up obvious sales leads, be seen as a ***connector of people.***
- ***Invite*** other delegates to different networking groups. Every networker needs a variety of groups, as they all deliver different things for you.
- Scrutinise all the business cards you collected and maintain a ***networking database*** with the data. Record where and when you met, as these are good icebreakers next time you make contact.
- Above all, arrange ***one-to-one meetings*** with other delegates and not just with people who are potential clients. These should typically be for 30 or 60 minutes and by the end both parties should know the following: -

  *Who they are and what they do*
  *What it is that they are looking for*
  *How they have agreed to help each other*

No matter how experienced the networkers are, everyone knows something that will be of use to the other – people, organisations, useful websites, useful business tools, meeting venues etc. One-to-one meetings are the only way to really drill down and find out what people do, and what help they need.

So that is my recommended route to effective networking – ***The Five Ps.***
***Preparation*** – treat networking meetings just as professionally as you would any other business meetings. Organise yourself and give yourself the best chance of success

***Performance*** – don’t just turn up, be proactive and really work the room
***Pitch*** – don’t just cram as many words as you can into the time you have been given, be memorable
***Patience*** – don’t regard networking as a “quick fix”, give each group time to work
***Persistence*** – follow up and build relationships for mutual gain

If you follow the Five Ps, doing all these things well and regularly, networking WILL work for you.

### *EFFECTIVE ONLINE NETWORKING*

Until March 2020, almost all business networking consisted of face-to-face events with lots of handshakes and business cards. Once the COVID-19 lockdown situation was imposed, it was no longer possible for physical meetings. Groups therefore converted very quickly to the use of online platforms like Zoom and Microsoft Teams. We all had to learn very swiftly how to use these new business tools – it probably would have happened anyway over about 5 years, but it became necessary to make that switch within a month!

Many of the points above apply equally to online and to physical face-to-face networking events. But here are a few things that online networkers can do to ensure that their online networking is effective: -

- The online networker should take care that their appearance on-screen is professional, not necessarily like a tailor’s dummy but at least looking as though they have made an effort. If you appear unkempt and scruffy on-screen, then that is what other networkers will think about your business. Good lighting can help here.

- Be aware of what other participants can see. If you are using a laptop, place it on a box or a stack of books, so that the laptop's camera is level with your eyes. If you lay it just on a table or desk, the other participants have a wonderful view up your nose!
- Remember that other participants can see you at all times, unless you have selected the "video off" setting. So, be careful not to make any embarrassing clothing adjustments in view of the camera!
- Use the background either to show your logo and contact details – or perhaps use a photo or image which is consistent with your product or service. Some meeting platforms (like Zoom) allow you to adjust the mirror image, so that words and pictures appear the right way round.
- Throughout the online meeting, it is important that each attendee appears to be taking a genuine interest in what other networkers have to say – so emails, text messages and online games should be ignored during the meeting. As a courtesy to the other people, avoid looking bored or distracted.
- It is advisable to prepare in advance a "script" which you can feed into the meeting's Chat box (using copy and paste). This should contain all your contact details as well as a clue as to the kind of help you need.
- How you sound is so important, so check before the meeting that your speakers and microphone are

working properly. Also, try to eliminate all unwanted background sounds – barking dogs, electric drills, radios etc.

- As with face-to-face networking, it is important that you rehearse your elevator pitch – and try to be memorable, without too much jargon. Use the allotted time but without speaking too quickly.
- If you are allowed to make presentations via a screen share facility, try them out with the organiser just before the meeting starts.
- Some meetings will include breakout rooms, where you meet with a small number of people. Try to avoid replicating your standard pitch and use the time instead to find out more about the other people in your "room".
- Keep an eye on the Chat box during the meeting in case other participants are trying to contact you – and always save the Chat facility just before the end of the meeting. There could well be some useful contact data in there.
- If the organiser does not issue lists of participants, you need to write down details during the meeting, sometimes adding data from the Chat box later. Soon after the meeting has finished, scrutinise the Chat box to see if anyone has requested a follow up meeting with you.

As with physical meetings, it is important to evaluate online networking groups, comparing the time and money spent against the benefits gained. They have the big advantage of not requiring long road journeys before and after the events – but they still take time and so should be reviewed regularly.

# PART 3

# INEFFECTIVE NETWORKING

"There are worse things in life than death. Have you ever spent an evening with an insurance salesman?" (Woody Allen)

"You are either part of the solution or part of the problem." (Anon)

Having discussed all the things you can do in order to ensure your business networking is effective, the converse also needs to be examined, in other words ***How Not To Network***. Over the years, I have seen some very slick operators on the networking circuit, taking advantage of every opportunity to promote their business and grow their list of useful contacts. I have also seen lots of people who have seen very poor returns from their networking - and of course they blame everything and everyone but themselves. These are the kind of mistakes made by bad networkers: -

***Treat Networking as a Selling Exercise*** – some people enter a networking meeting and all they can see is a roomful of potential customers, almost like a hunter surveying its prey. They do not listen to what other people have to say, they just want to deliver their sales message while pinning their victims up against the wall. They show you images on their tablets and often dish out unwieldy A4 folders to take away. The following morning, they are on the phone to you, just checking if you have had chance to consider their irresistible proposition. This aggressive attitude just turns other networkers off and the "hunter" is given a wide berth thereafter. This attitude is probably the most common cause of networking failure.

***Fail to Prepare*** – networking is often an "out of hours" activity, sometimes over breakfast, lunch or evening meal. It can be fun and sometimes overlaps into delegates' social lives. Many small business owners work on their own and welcome the human contact they experience at networking events. As a result of this, networking can be misconstrued as being a less than serious activity and less important than more formal activities. Delegates can therefore fall into the trap of letting their preparation slip, for instance: -

- They don't check on the venue or the time, arriving dishevelled, flustered and late. This creates a very negative impression of the networkers and their businesses
- They don't check on the format of the meeting, so they are surprised when they have less time (or more time) to speak
- They don't clarify their objectives, so they can't measure the outcome
- They don't take enough business cards with them – perhaps the greatest crime in the networking world

***Keep to Themselves*** – instead of proactively working the room, some networkers stay on their own and miss a great opportunity. This often occurs with new networkers – but if they don't change their ways they will find it a less than successful experience. And they just might be lost to the networking world.

***Stay with their Pals*** – let me be controversial here and state that the worst culprits for this networking crime are usually accountants, bankers and solicitors – but others can sometimes be just as bad. These people arrive with their colleagues, drink coffee with their colleagues and leave with their colleagues. They make no attempt to engage with anyone else and they go back to the office having achieved nothing. What a waste of time!

***Don't Bother to Work on their Pitch*** – delivering a memorable pitch is so important at networking events but some people just don't give it the attention it deserves.

Whilst scratching their chair across the floor, they mumble their name then they deliver a standard announcement, with far too many words packed into the allocated time. They use abbreviations and jargon no-one else can understand and don't clarify what exactly they are looking for. And finally, they don't bother to check with anyone whether their message has come across. As a result, no other networkers understand enough to pass on the information.

***Become Frustrated when Immediate Leads do not Appear*** – it often takes a while for networking activity to result in invoiced sales but some networkers do not understand this. Instead, they expect prospective customers to come knocking on their door the morning after each event. Sometimes this can happen because the business' accountant wants to see early value for money. If expectations are not managed, these networkers disappear from the circuit.

***Fail to Follow Up*** – this is probably the worst thing a networker can get wrong. Having given up time (and probably money), passed business cards to all and sundry, delivered a well-prepared pitch and generally promoted the business well, the networker then fails to build upon the foundations laid. There are no phone calls, no emails, no social media interactions and no one-to-one meetings. What a waste of time!

When the networking process appears not to have worked, the networkers blame everyone else, or they blame the process. In every one of the above cases, the bad networkers themselves are to blame. With help and advice from networking group leaders, some of them can be turned around – but only if they are prepared to listen.

***Fail to Create a Positive Online Presence*** – since early 2020, the majority of business networking has been online and much of our networking going forwards will be via an increasing number of online meeting platforms. Some of the points I have made above equally apply to online and physical face-to-face networking but there are a number of areas where online networkers get things wrong: -

- Not standing the laptop on something to raise the camera to eye level, which means that the other attendees get a wonderful view up your nose!
- Not eliminating the default "mirror" view which makes printed materials or pictures behind you appear the wrong way round.
- Not having enough lighting in the room which gives the impression of working from a dungeon.
- Failing to remove distractions from the background (children, pets, co-workers).
- Not appearing interested, attentive and ready to help during the other participants' elevator pitches.
- Failing to prepare presentations which will be used via a screen-sharing facility. This can cause embarrassing periods of silence whilst being fixed during the meeting.
- Not preparing appropriate text before the meeting (with all your contact details and identification of what you are seeking) so that you can just copy and paste it into the meeting's Chat facility.
- Preparing too much text, so that the Chat box is overwhelmed.
- Not saving the Chat before the meeting ends.

- Not checking with the group organiser how they could improve their performance – instead blaming the group, the other delegates and the process. As with physical networking, ineffective online networking is nearly always the fault of the networker.

# PART 4

# BUILDING, GROWING & MAINTAINING A NETWORKING CLUB

"Business is a combination of war and sport." (André Maurois)

Questioner – "what is two and two?" Lord Grade – "buying or selling?"

Many networking groups are run by business people in their spare time and, as long as those people get regular and substantial help from a number of the members, the group can perform very successfully. Some groups are very informal, with relatively unstructured meetings and there is nothing wrong with that, if that is what the members want. But the following guidance is based on these premises: -

- The networking club is a significant (perhaps sole) business interest of the person(s) running it
- The club operates on the basis of chargeable memberships
- The members are discerning customers who demand good value from their membership
- The members are business people who are looking for self-development just as much as making new contacts
- It is intended to establish a brand and a reputation which may facilitate a subsequent franchising operation

**Research**

Before any decisions are made, it is important to fully research the market. Which other groups operate, who are their members, when do they meet, where do they meet, what do they charge and how are their meetings formatted? It would make sense to visit as many other groups' events as possible to get a full picture. Those groups' members should be asked what they like and dislike, to understand what gaps exist.
The business networking group you are seeking to create is like any other business – for it to be successful, you

must offer something which is better or different, preferably both. You can only do this once you understand what other players in the market are doing.

**Fundamentals**

*Timing* – this is one of the most important decisions you will make. Will you organise meetings in the morning, at lunchtime or in the evening? Which days of the week will you choose? Will you use a mix of these options? What other potentially-conflicting events must you avoid? You cannot please everyone, so whatever combination you go for, there will always be someone who cannot come because it clashes with something else.
Regularity is important, so decide what your policy will be with regard to breaks – for instance if your normal meeting date coincides with a bank holiday, will you delay things by a day, by a week or what? Will you meet every 2 weeks or, say, the first and third Wednesdays? Will it be the fourth Thursday or the last Thursday?
When you are launching a new group, you might just get the timing wrong. Take feedback from the members and of course from people who are unable to attend, and if you have to tweak or compromise things, then so be it.

*Format* – as you will see from the second half of this book, I have always been a great advocate of variety at networking events and I tried very hard not to be too predictable or repetitive. But some groups prefer to use pretty much the same agenda, in the same order, every time they meet. There is no right or wrong way, but I recommend that you leave yourself the flexibility to do something different as often as the members want. If you are planning to provide food and drink, will this be at the

very beginning or maybe during a half-time break? Will it be a conventional meal or a buffet? What opportunities will you give attendees to pitch their businesses? Will you have a formal referrals section?
Thinking closely about the format of your meetings is where you can create a USP for your group – what can you do that no competitors are doing?

*Pricing and Positioning* – many of the decisions you make will be governed by where you are positioning your group. Compared to other networking groups, will you be up-market, somewhere in the middle, or no-frills? To a certain extent, your pricing model will depend on "food or no food", the choice of venue and who your target members are. And when it comes to actual numbers, my old white goods experience taught me that if you want to get below a psychological price threshold, there is no need to go too far below – so £29 is good enough to get under £30, you don't need to go in at £25. Consider annual versus monthly pricing and also a "pay on the door" option. Remember that your business needs to be profitable, so you need to find that sweet spot which gives the members great value for money and which makes it all worthwhile for you.

*Venue* – having decided where you are going to position your club, having decided what time of day you are going to meet and having decided whether you will provide food or not, you then have to select an appropriate venue for your meetings. Obviously the venue needs to be consistent with where you have positioned the club and some of the items you must consider are (a) location and accessibility, (b) car parking, (c) meeting room facilities, (d) availability

of screens, projectors, flipcharts, (e) smartness and cleanliness and (f) quality of food and drink.
Having thrown all of those things into the mix, you can then compare prices. You will get far better prices from venues if you promise a guaranteed minimum number of heads per meeting and maybe six or twelve months block bookings.

*Standards and House Rules* – networking events are often held outside of office hours and can be interpreted as being less than serious affairs, more fun and social than business. Whilst every attempt should be made to ensure that all participants enjoy themselves, you should leave folks in no doubt that your events are professional business activities which are vital elements within a marketing strategy. Whilst this list is far from exhaustive, here are some of the things you need to consider if you are to establish your own way of working: -

- From the outset, ensure that your meetings start on time and keep to the same times for breaks and closures. Encourage delegates to arrive on time but set an example yourself. Also, if delegates or guest speakers are given an allotted time in which to speak, be seen to be strict and consistent.
- I recommend a ban on bad language, with the wrong-doers being asked to contribute into a charity box. This is not a severe punishment, but it makes the point that your club is a professional environment.
- I am not sure that you can ban alcoholic drinks, but you should certainly discourage it. Would anyone really take a pint of beer into any other business

meeting? Post-meeting gatherings in the bar are fine, though.
- Avoid poor spelling and poor grammar on every document produced in the name of the club (announcements, invitations, delegate lists, emails, slides, website, social media etc). Such errors can look so amateurish and can conflict with the positioning of the club.
- It is more practical to have a literature table at the side of the networking room, rather than allowing delegates to swamp each table with flyers and samples.
- You need to have a policy on allowing delegates to use pull-up banners at your meetings. Should anyone be allowed, just sponsors, just speakers, or just charities?

*Exclusivity* – some networking clubs allow any number of businesses from the same business sector to join, and they sell this as a benefit of joining. Other groups only allow one business from each sector to join (a "lockout") and this also is sold as a benefit of joining. Both types of club have a role to play, but it is really important that you establish up front exactly what your club's policy is on exclusivity.

**Branding and PR**

As with all businesses, it is important that you develop a strong brand for your club, and some of the things above about positioning and standards will go a long way towards helping to build that brand. We will look in a while at retaining existing customers and that too will play a part in the building of the brand.

*Name* – take your time, do your homework and look to the future when deciding upon the name of your group. The inclusion of your city or county in the name will make future expansion and possible franchising difficult. Do not use names which are similar to other networking groups, nor any names which may suggest associations with other businesses (so don't use "Barclays Business Club" or "Harrods Networking" for instance). Check out registered names at Companies House, registered trademarks, the availability of appropriate domain names and social media handles. Don't rush into things because it can be costly to be forced into changing your name later.

*Logo, House Style, USPs* – once you have named your group, take advice on how you should present that group. You may well already know people who can help you – graphic designers, website designers, printers and PR specialists. Maybe you could negotiate a deal whereby such businesses could provide their services for little or no cost, in exchange for so many months of free membership. They may even just do the work knowing that you will give them a regular mention. Don't be afraid to ask! When choosing logos and house colours, avoid any confusion with similar groups and avoid any implied association with other businesses.
Identifying your USPs can be tricky – but you must have something which makes you stand out from the rest, so use some superlatives. For a little while you can claim to be the newest or freshest, and then the fastest-growing group but then you need to think. What are you – the most innovative, the most varied, the most thought-provoking,

the most exciting? Do you have the best speakers, the best food, the best value for money package?

*Materials* – to help spread your name, advertise your brand and reward members for joining. You should look at issuing branded items, the quality of which must be consistent with your positioning. Having your brand on poor quality merchandise does you no good at all, so try not to go down that route. Things you could consider are folders with writing pads and branded pens, name badges, mugs, drink mats, mouse mats, calendars – things that are used regularly. You will need to think also about items that you will use yourself when promoting your group at other events – pull-up banners, simple leaflets or flyers, videos and business cards.

*Website* – it is crucially important that you have someone produce and maintain a professional website for you. After picking up your business card, the first contact someone has with you is via your website, so make sure it creates the right first impression – it must look professional, welcoming and be easy to navigate. It should include: -

- Mission statement, to clarify what potential members can expect to receive from their membership – this could be a block of text or a brief spoken introduction on video
- Details of venues, times of meetings, calendar of events
- Videos of actual meetings plus interviews with satisfied members
- Lists of members, probably with website links and contact phone numbers
- Privacy statement and Ts & Cs

- And, finally, a call to action – either a box in which to request information or actual registration for an event

*App* – nowadays it is becoming essential to have someone create an App for your club. This enables members to easily access data on the club, its members and its events.

*Social Media* – as someone looking to establish a networking group, it is essential that you are seen to be spreading the networking word via social media. Physical face-to-face networking is an important element within a business' marketing strategy – and so is a social media presence. The new networking group, and its leader, should be seen to be very active on social media in order to drive potential members to the website and ultimately to actual meetings. Regular posts or articles can help to establish the group leader as a networking "expert". If necessary, the club's social media activity can be run by a third party – almost certainly a member of the club. Once meetings are up and running, reference to the club's handles and links should be given out at every opportunity.

**Getting Started**

Having conducted lots of research and decided upon your proposition, positioning, identity and USPs, it is time to take a big breath and launch your new networking club to the business community. You only get one chance to make a good first impression, so you need to make sure everything is in place beforehand. Avoid the temptation to rush in and don't flag up your intentions to your competitors too soon, of course.

*Launch Event* – your first event should be free of charge, it should showcase some of the things people are going to see at the regular events and it should feature an inspiring guest speaker. And people will expect to be fed. Professional literature should be available – leaflets, business cards, introductory letters, list of events, list of delegates, table numbers etc. And it ought to take place at the venue you plan to use regularly.

*Presentations* – without overdoing Powerpoint, your introductory presentations should be supported by professional slides and videos.

*Introductory Offers* – getting new members signed up is obviously a priority, so think about what introductory offers could be made in order to help them make a decision. These might include discount off the first year's membership if signed up by a certain date, initial 3 months free membership, access to an exclusive grade of membership ("founder members", "inaugural members" etc), free sponsorship spots etc. I am a great believer in delegates coming once to a free meeting, so that they can see and feel the product for themselves, but I think they should pay thereafter. You could consider a "pack" of special offers from likely first members as thanks to your first attendees.

*Guarantees* – any business worth its salt should be able to stand behind a "money back" promise, and networking groups are no different. When making such an offer, you should ensure that the member has actually made a decent effort to make it work, insisting on a minimum number of attendances in the year and stating that an interim review meeting must take place. Having a guarantee in place makes the signing up of new members so much easier.

*Application forms, direct debit mandates etc* – it is imperative that you always have close at hand those pieces of paper which convert prospects into members, so these must be available for the launch meeting and for every subsequent follow-up meeting with prospective members.

*Agreements, Ts & Cs* – the new membership application form should incorporate the actual agreement between the two parties (taking advice to ensure there are no data protection issues) and a copy of your Terms and Conditions should be given to the new members with their copy of the Application/Agreement document.

*Publicity* – we have already looked at the importance of social media and this will really come into its own when it comes to advertising your launch event. But don't just leave it to social media – prepare a Press Release, phone the local business press (hard copy and digital), invite the local press to the launch event, phone the local radio, contact those business organisations which issue regular newsletters and bulletins. And look at the cost of actually using a PR firm to do these things for you.

*Other networking groups* – some networking groups may see you as a competitor who is trying to steal some of their share of the market. But the vast majority will adopt a more grown-up attitude and will openly help you to establish your new group. In order to get this level of co-operation, you need to be open and up-front with them, so don't let them find out about you from others.

Just attending other networking meetings (passing your cards, distributing your flyers, delivering your pitches) will help you to publicise the birth of your club. But these other groups may also allow you to make announcements about your meetings. If they do, you should reciprocate and give them a mention at your events.
Try very hard to treat other networking groups as collaborators rather than competitors – they are not all the same and they each bring something different to the party.

*Target businesses and sectors* – no potential member wants to join a club which only has accountants, estate agents or website designers. Instead, they want to join a club which has a wide variety of businesses – different sizes and different sectors. So, when you are drawing up a list of potential delegates for your launch meeting, work hard to develop a really varied list. And of course, once the club is established, you will need to constantly monitor the type of members you have.

**Finding New Members**

Running a business (any business) is very simple. It involves finding customers, retaining customers and managing cash. So, how are you going to find prospective new members for your club?

*Networking groups* – you need to put some hours in when it comes to visiting and befriending other networking groups, even if it costs money to attend them. This is the low-hanging fruit, the delegates have already grasped the principle of networking, you just need to persuade them to try your group as well. Make it clear that you want them to attend yours as well as the one they are at, don't try to entice them to your club instead of the other one. Out of courtesy, when attending other clubs, present your USPs as things which are different and not necessarily better. When these people eventually turn up at one of your meetings, tell everyone at your club where you met them, thus returning the compliment to the other club.

*Expos, Conferences, Seminars* – I am a great believer that all gatherings of business people are potential networking opportunities, so you must go along with that in mind. Do not forget your business cards, flyers and (if they are allowed) pull-up banners. Prepare a fairly brief pitch to deliver either one-to-one or to a table of delegates. But be careful – at events which are not advertised as networking events, not everyone wants to network so you must respect that and perhaps be a little more low-key. But at least try to get business cards for subsequent following-up.

*Social Media* – you can use the various social media platforms in a number of ways: -
Mention general details of your club
Announce forthcoming events
Praise or recommend your members – and others you have met on the networking circuit
Share your members' posts
Thank your speakers and link to their websites
Post brief articles including best networking practices, so be seen as a networking "expert"
Absolutely avoid politics, controversies and any criticism of other business groups
Include your contact details and links to your website

*Press* – having used the facilities of the press to publicise your initial launch event, be proactive and work with them to reach potential new members. Try to contribute regular articles about business networking, with photographs of your club in action. And don't forget to invite the press to any anniversaries or special events.

*Incentives* – the biggest challenge is to get potential members to come along and try one of your meetings. Once they have experienced a meeting and seen what they can take away, it is relatively easy to sign people up – if it is the right format, timing and cost for them. The biggest incentive for people to come in the first place is if the meeting is free, because they have nothing to lose. If you have chosen the venue, the timing and the food well, then those should be incentive enough.

**Retaining Members**

Too many businesses become obsessed with finding new customers, they become complacent, and then they find that they are losing existing customers. Retaining customers is vital if your networking group is to survive and thrive. It must be an ongoing priority in your business. So, what should you do to ensure you keep your members?

*Induction* – once you have signed members up, it is important that they are helped to get as much from their membership as possible. And then they will stay with you. You should hold regular (every 4 or 6 weeks) induction sessions, at which the new members are taught how to use their membership. I recommend daytime sessions of about 2 hours, with an agenda something like this: -

- Elevator pitches with a difference, perhaps 2 minutes on how they have got to where they are now
- History of the club
- Profile of the club – number of members, business sectors covered
- Meeting details – timings, ground rules, different formats
- Structuring of elevator pitches
- How to use the club's website and social media
- How to use the club's members (stressing the need for regular contact and one-to-one meetings)

*Regular feedback* – you need to know which formats are working, what members like and dislike, what members would like in addition to what you give them and you need to recognise if any members are unhappy and likely to leave your group. There are several things you can do to check how satisfied your members are: -
One-to-one sessions before your regular meetings, after other networking groups' meetings, in a coffee shop or in a hotel bar.
Small group sessions (maybe 5 or 6 members), perhaps over lunch.
Questionnaires handed out at your regular meetings.
Telephoned questionnaires, using outside specialists.
The fact that you are taking the trouble to invite members' feedback will in itself be well received. You get to find out what members think and you can nip in the bud any simmering unrest.

*Regular reviews* – as well as specific questions on formats etc, as part of your guarantee you should make yourself available to meet individual members and discuss the value for money they are receiving. You can agree all the things that can be done (almost all of which will be for them to do) in order for them to get more out of their membership.

*Variety* – members leave networking groups if they feel that the groups are becoming stale. Doing the same things over and over again will result in members looking elsewhere for inspiration. Throwing in lots of variety will constantly refresh the club and ensure that members do not get bored. Later in this book, we will look at the many ways in which variety can be injected.

*Maintaining standards* – when we looked at starting a club, we said that it was important to establish some ground rules regarding punctuality, bad language, alcohol etc. To ensure that you retain your members, you need to be consistent and maintain those standards.

*"Love"* – your club members are your customers, so they need to feel valued and appreciated. I was always fine at developing business conversations with members, but it was my wife, Diana, who remembered which members had poorly arms, whose kids were doing exams and whose car had broken down after our last meeting. Try to take an interest in the members themselves and not just their businesses.

*Credit control* – being blunt about things, the real reason for retaining members is so that they continue to pay for their membership. Without fees coming in, there will be no club. It is important therefore that you keep a close eye on payments. Politely chase overdue payments as soon as they slip past their due date and let it be known that you are no "soft touch". However, when a member has a short-term cashflow issue, a sympathetic gesture can help to build loyalty.

*Exit interviews* – as with all businesses, it is important to understand why customers have chosen not to continue buying from you. I recommend that, as soon as you hear that a member is leaving, meet them for a coffee and take feedback from them – what they liked, what they disliked, why they are leaving. Often it is just a change in their circumstances but if something in the club needs changing, then you need to know about it.

**Branching Out**

The simplest way to grow your club is, of course, to keep on signing up new members. But if you just concentrate on growing the number of members, there is a chance that you could end up with very large meetings. The whole thing then becomes unwieldy and unfortunately the quality of members' experiences can be adversely affected. The largest networking meeting I organised had 91 attendees and, with hindsight, that was just a bit too cosy!
There are, however, a number of other ways in which you can grow your networking business. When going ahead with any of these, it is important that you "keep your eye on the ball" and avoid neglecting what you have already established. Don't take on anything new if it means compromising your existing club.

*Additional events* – as well as continuing with your core operation, you could introduce other events (perhaps on different days, at different times of the day and targeted at different business types). Some ideas might include: -

- Networking events for new businesses
- Networking events for women
- Joint networking events with other groups
- Smaller, brainstorming groups
- Training events, if possible, facilitated by members of the group
- Golf tournaments
- Bowling evenings
- Networking events at horse racing, greyhounds, speedway meetings etc

Alternatively, you could occasionally take your normal meeting and stage it at the premises of one of your members

*Additional venues* – this involves replicating your core club and doing exactly the same in a different place. This could be at a second venue in the same city or it could be in a completely different place. All of the points made about establishing a new club apply here, except that you have a proven model as an example. Before launching a new location, you need to consider these items: -
What sort of geographical challenge is presented?
Who will do the recruiting, organising, facilitating, administering and following-up?
Will pricing and benefits be identical between the old and new clubs?
Will membership include access to both clubs?

*Trademarking* – as you expand and your clubs become well known, there is an increasing risk of being copied and plagiarised. To prevent this from happening, it makes sense to trademark your name, or logo, or house style, or all of these. Of course, it takes time and money to secure a trademark but you leave yourself wide open if you fail to do so. My advice is to use a recognised patent attorney – this may seem expensive but it is the peace of mind that you are paying for.

*Franchising* – if you are expanding within your existing city, or into a neighbouring city, you may well be able to handle it all yourself. I successfully ran clubs in Lincoln and Peterborough because I lived in between the two locations. But if you are planning to expand into cities farther afield, you should consider setting up franchising operations. This is where the brand name, style, format, materials and culture are exactly the same as in your core club – but you are not the person running it. Certainly, all the training, advice and guidance is provided by you, but all the legwork is done by your franchisee. Therefore, the income has to be allocated across both parties. This is not a definitive list, but areas to consider when setting up a franchise operation include: -

- You must retain absolute control over the use of your logos, styling, marketing materials and website
- You must be prepared to put in many hours of training
- The franchisee must be encouraged to provide feedback, ideas and recommendations
- The financials must be fair to both parties. An unrewarded franchisee will not be motivated
- The arrangement must be formalised by an official Franchising Agreement

*Merger and Takeover* – rather than try to build another club in a new city, it may be appropriate to acquire or merge with an organisation which is already established there. In the case of a merger, it will only work if the positioning of both businesses is similar.

**Takeaway**

Many people have wrongfully assumed that it is easy to set up a business networking club – and that is why so many have come and gone over the years. For a club to succeed, you need to be positive, dedicated and organised. There will be many disappointments along the way, as people unexpectedly let you down. But you will also be pleasantly surprised to discover new business relationships, new business techniques and lasting personal friendships. There will be a really warm glow when you hear of two businesses who had been introduced by you and who are now successfully working together. Getting a reputation as a "connector of people" is no bad thing.

# PART 5

# PRESENTATIONS ON THE SUBJECT OF NETWORKING

"Never be afraid to try something new. Remember, amateurs built the Ark, professionals built the Titanic." (Anon)

"A fool and his money are soon parted. What I want to know is how they got together in the first place." (Cyril Fletcher)

When establishing or growing your networking group, it does you no harm at all to be recognised as a networking expert. As well as by blogging and writing social media posts, you can enhance this reputation by delivering a range of presentations on the subject of networking. During these presentations you can teach people things that they just didn't know about networking, but you can also give them a taster of what to expect at one of your meetings.

These presentations can be delivered in speaker slots for other networking groups, as training modules for companies, for groups of students and at general business expo/conference events. People like the Institute of Directors, the local Chambers of Commerce and the FSB all welcome guest speakers so you should have no qualms about offering your services to them. Unfortunately, you are unlikely to get paid for this, so just regard it as a marketing investment.

It makes sense to keep some of these presentations up your sleeve in case (a) the speaker at one of your own events does not show up or (b) you turn up at someone else's event and you are asked if you can "fill in" at short notice.

This section includes presentations which can take anything between 10 minutes and 90 minutes, depending upon how many "Ice-Breaker" activities are used in between slides. Part 6 of this book includes a number of "Ice-Breakers" which can be slotted in to amplify certain points. I have shown the content in a series of lists, but in practice these would be presented via a series of Powerpoint slides, illustrated with appropriate pictures, images, sound effects and animations. Make sure any slides you use are well branded and, if appropriate, present your slides using your club's house colours.

The presentations included in this section are: -

a) Destroying The Myths Of Networking
b) Effective Online Networking
c) Five Ps Of Networking
d) Hey, It's Networking Not Selling!
e) Is Your Networking NOT Working?
f) Networking Encyclopaedia
g) Networking Jungle
h) Ten Commandments Of Networking
i) Three Biggest Mistakes Of Networking
j) Working The Room

## PART 5 (a) – Destroying The Myths Of Networking

This presentation is aimed at inexperienced networkers who usually have a number of pre-conceived fears of networking. It seeks to identify the fears that people have about networking and it then seeks to destroy those myths via a series of "Ice-Breaker" activities (see Part 6).

The opening slide, entitled **"The Myths Of Networking",** lists those items which are known to put people off networking

- It is just a casual activity
- It is a frightening ordeal
- It is hard to approach people
- It is difficult to break the ice
- It is just selling
- It can be hard to get rid of "bores"
- It is tough working out what to say
- It can be a problem following-up

The rest of the presentation consists of slides and physical activities which address each of these "myths"

The next slide, entitled **"Casual Activity?",** lists the important items of preparation required before a networking event

Check Beforehand

- Venue & Time
- Format
- Other Attendees
- Dress Code
- Objectives

"Must Take" Items

- Business Cards
- Pen & Notebook
- Flyers & Leaflets
- Banners
- Diary

The takeaway at the foot of the slide states "Serious Business Activity, Nothing Casual"

The next slide is entitled **"Frightening Ordeal?"** and it accompanies the "Birthday Line" ice-breaker

The next slide is entitled **"Hard To Approach People?"** It starts by making the point that it is important to abandon colleagues at the door and then lists the five types of group to be approached

- Singletons
- Closed 2s
- Open 2s
- Open 3s
- Groups

Volunteers are "appointed" so that you can demonstrate the different approach techniques

The next slide, entitled **"Difficult To Break The Ice?"**, contains a list of suggested ways of breaking the ice

- Weather
- First time here?
- Had a good journey?
- Can you introduce me?
- Ask them about themselves
- Use "open" questions

The next slide is entitled **"Just Selling?"** and it is used while the "Present And Back" icebreaker is run. This demonstrated the importance of listening in networking. The takeaway line at the foot of the slide reads "Networking Is Marketing, NOT Selling

The next slide is entitled **"Getting Rid Of Bores?"** and it lists 4 ways of moving people on

- Tea/Coffee
- Toilet
- Tense Change ("it has been nice talking with you" or "it was good to meet you")
- Pass On To A "Friend" (and then leg it!)

Volunteers are called up to demonstrate these points

The next slide is entitled **"Don't Know What To Say?"** and it includes a tongue-in-cheek list of points made in poor elevator pitches

- This is me
- This is a long list of what I do
- This is a load of jargon with lots of mysterious abbreviations
- This is how long I have done it
- Let me know if you want to buy
- And this is me again

The next slide is entitled **"What Can You Remember?"** and is followed by the "Thanks For The Memory" activity

After that activity, another slide called **"Don't Know What To Say?"** includes the correct way of making a pitch

- Name
- BENEFIT of what I do
- How I do it
- My clients
- Help I need
- Name again

The final slide is called **“Problem Following Up?”** and includes a list of ways in which networkers can follow up

- “To Do” list before leaving the event
- Takes 4-7 contacts before being recommended
- Phone, E-Mail, Social Media
- Newsletter, Blog etc
- “Dignified Stalking”

The takeaway at the foot of the slide states “Be Patient But Persistent”

The presentation concludes by repeating the original list of “Myths” and confirming that they have all been destroyed by the various activities and discussions.

## PART 5 (b) – Effective Online Networking

This brief presentation illustrates the similarities and the differences when comparing face-to-face networking with online networking and should incorporate appropriate screenshots to make points. There are also a number of amusing YouTube examples of how NOT to network online – these can be added to the presentation where appropriate.

Before March 2020, online networking groups were very few and far between. Almost all networking events consisted of people physically meeting other people in order to develop mutually-beneficial business relationships. But then the first COVID phase hit us hard, and we were told we couldn't congregate to hold indoor business meetings. Some networking groups folded, but most of them quickly changed direction and set up online meetings via facilities like Zoom, Microsoft Teams etc. There is no doubt that online networking would have developed anyway, perhaps over a period of 5 years – instead, we all had to make that transition within a few weeks!

This presentation identifies the similarities, the differences and what networkers need to do in order for their online networking to be effective.

First Slide, entitled "**Networking Principles Which Also Apply Online**"

- Only one opportunity to make a good first impression
- Be punctual, even early

- Look and act professionally
- Prepare your pitch beforehand and rehearse it
- Use visual props for effect
- Follow up promptly after meetings

Second Slide, entitled "**Differences Between Physical and Online Networking**"

- Cost
- Dress Code
- Background
- Interruptions and Distractions
- Loss of Internet or phone signal

Third Slide, entitled "**Online Networking – What Must You Do?"**

- Check that you have the joining link the day before your meeting starts
- Check your camera and sound work
- Check the view others have of you
- Avoid looking slovenly, scruffy or unprofessional
- If presenting, check your slides with the organiser beforehand
- Look attentive while others are presenting
- Use the chat box facility to share contact details
- Use the chat box facility to save other delegates' details
- Compile list of attendees (unless organiser provides one)

## PART 5 (c) – Five Ps Of Networking

This presentation covers the main principles of effective networking and can take anything between ten minutes and an hour, depending upon which other activities are included. The content is suitable for new or experienced networkers.

The first slide is entitled "**5 Ps Of Networking**" and merely lists what the 5 Ps are: -

1. Preparation
2. Performance
3. Pitch
4. Patience
5. Persistence

The next slide is entitled "**1. Preparation**" and is broken down into two columns

Check Beforehand

- Venue & Time
- Format
- Other Attendees
- Dress Code
- Cost
- Attendees
- Objectives

"Must Take" Items

- Badge
- Business Cards
- Notes & Prompts
- Pen & Notebook
- Flyers & Leaflets
- Banners
- Diary

The next slide is entitled "**2. Performance**" and covers the following practical advice

- Arrive early and work the room
- Don't stay with the same people
- Keep cool and hydrated
- Introduce others and get yourself introduced

- Ask questions and then take a keen interest
- Make connections and do not blatantly sell
- Spend more time listening than talking
- Collect business cards and record actions
- Linger afterwards, don't rush away

The next slide is entitled "**3. Pitch**" and gives the following advice

- Understand the format
- Prepare your pitch
- Rehearse your pitch
- Keep hydrated
- Avoid speaking quickly
- Be clear and concise

The next slide is also entitled "**3. Pitch**" and gives advice on how to structure an elevator pitch

- Clearly say the name of you and your business
- Stress the benefit of what you do
- Explain what you do – simply and without jargon
- Do something visual
- Give examples of the type of customer you have
- Indicate what you are looking for
- Remind people of who you are again

The next slide is entitled "**4. Patience**" and covers

- Networking is not a "quick fix"
- Manage your expectations
- Between 4 and 7 contacts are necessary
- Any new group must be given time to work
- Avoid appearing pushy or impatient
- Maintain occasional contact

The penultimate slide is entitled "**5. Persistence**" and covers how to follow up and stay in touch

- Compile a list of actions after every networking event
- Follow up promptly, while things are fresh, but without appearing desperate
- Do all the things you have promised to do
- Invite new contacts to other networking events
- Establish yourself as a connector of people
- Arrange one-to-one meetings for further understanding
- Maintain a database of contacts

And the final slide contains the 5 Ps, plus one surprise

1. Preparation – don't sell, be early, take props
2. Performance – work the room
3. Pitch – be clear, concise and memorable
4. Patience – it is not a "quick fix"
5. Persistence – follow up & build relationships
6. Provide more than you promised

## PART 5 (d) – Hey, It's Networking, Not Selling

This is a very brief presentation, designed to fill a ten minutes spot at your own or other people's events. It tackles probably the biggest single reason why some folks don't get much from their networking – the salesman's mindset.

The first slide is entitled "**Networkers' 3 Biggest Mistakes**" and lists the following

- They fail to prepare
- They fail to follow up
- They think it is selling

The next slide is entitled "**What It Is Not**" and covers

- Networking is not "meet the buyer"
- Networking is not a room full of hot leads
- Networking is not a room full of folks with order pads
- Networking is NOT selling

The next slide is entitled "**What It Is**" and lists

- Networking is raising profile
- Networking is earning credibility
- Networking is creating or establishing a brand
- Networking is marketing

The next slide is entitled "**How Not To Do It**" and lists

- Don't pin people up against the wall
- Don't monopolise the conversation
- Don't blatantly sell to networkers
- Don't thrust leaflets under people's noses

The next slide is entitled “**Ask For Help, Not Orders**”

- Explain who you are and what you do
- Explain the types of business you are looking for
- Ask for help, advice and introductions

The final slide is a summary of the points already made, entitled “**Hey, It’s Networking, Not Selling**”

- Don’t go with the wrong mindset
- Don’t ask leading questions
- Don’t let folks think they are being sold to
- Don’t pin people to the wall
- Don’t monopolise conversations
- Seek to earn trust and build relationships
- Make it clear you are looking for help

## PART 5 (e) – Is Your Networking NOT Working?

This brief presentation identifies the reasons why networking appears to be not working for some people. Whenever people say to me that networking does not work, I am tempted to say "networking DOES work but you obviously DON'T" but then I bite my tongue and try to explore the ways in which they can improve. Whenever making this presentation it is worth starting out by telling the delegates that if their networking isn't working: -

- It is not the fault of the organisers
- It is not the fault of the other delegates
- It is not the fault of everyone else under the sun

At the end of the presentation I have used a large picture of a finger pointing back at the viewer – so that they are in no doubt whose fault it is!

The first slide includes a picture of a typical hard-selling "spiv" and lists the comments often made by such people: -

- I didn't get any orders
- I didn't pick up any leads
- There was no-one there I could sell to
- The people there weren't very receptive

The second slide then lists **what networking is NOT**: -

- "Meet The Buyer"
- Room full of warmed up clients
- Guaranteed sales leads
- Group of people with order pads

The next slide explains **what networking CAN be**: -

- Opportunity to pick up sales leads
- Chance to meet new suppliers
- Contact with advisers and experts
- Forming of collaborations
- Development of business owner and staff
- Raining of profile

The next slide makes the point that "Networking Is Not Selling, Networking Is Marketing"

The next slide gives guidance on **how to prepare for each event**: -
Check Beforehand

- Venue & Time
- Format
- Other Attendees
- Dress Code
- Cost
- Attendees
- Objectives

"Must Take" Items

- Badge
- Business Cards
- Notes & Prompts
- Pen & Notebook
- Flyers & Leaflets
- Banners
- Diary

The next slide contains tips on "**Making Good Use Of Your Time**"

- Arrive early but linger afterwards
- Don't stick with the same people
- Introduce and get introduced
- Ask questions & take an interest
- Make connections, don't just sell
- Collect business cards & make notes

The next slide suggests a format for **an effective "elevator pitch"**

- This my NAME and business
- This is the BENEFIT of what I do
- This is HOW I do it
- Just like I have for this PERSON
- And this is my NAME again

The next slide makes points regarding **the need to be patient**

- It takes 4 to 7 contacts before you get recommended
- Every group must be given the chance to work
- You should maintain polite but regular contact

The next slide reminds delegates **how to follow-up**

- Write down action points before leaving
- Get in touch soon
- Do whatever you have promised
- Follow up all leads
- Invite delegates to other events
- Maintain a database of contacts
- Observe data protection permissions

The penultimate slide confirms the key points of **Effective Networking**

- Regard it as Marketing not Selling
- Plan and Prepare
- Use the room and be Memorable
- Always, Always, Always Follow Up
- And …. work very hard at it

The final slide asks the question **"If Your Networking Is NOT Working …. Whose Fault Is It?"**
And then a large finger is revealed, pointing back at the viewer

## PART 5 (f) – Networking Encyclopaedia

This presentation can take as long as you want and it can be delivered to your own networking group (especially if you need to fill in for an absent speaker) or at other meetings where they are looking for a 20-30 minutes standalone presentation.

It basically carves up the alphabet and allocates a networking discussion point (or piece of advice) to each letter. You can of course use each letter entirely as you wish and you can introduce little activities to amplify the points being made.

Here is a suggested list: -

A Arrive Early
B Business Cards
C Check Details
D Don't Get Bogged Down
E Elevator Pitch
F Follow Up
G Give It Chance To Work
H Hot List
I Introductions
J Joint Opportunities
K Keep Cool & Hydrated
L Listening
M "Must Take" Items
N NOT Selling
O Objectives
P Persistence
Q Questioning
R Referrals

| | |
|---|---|
| S | Stay Behind At The End |
| T | Targets |
| U | USP |
| V | Venue |
| W | Work The Room |
| X | Xtend Invitations |
| Y | You |
| Z | Zero Hour |

## PART 5 (g) – Networking Jungle

This presentation seeks to represent networkers as animals, recognisable from their networking behaviour. It can take as long as you have, either a 20 minutes blast or a full hour with activities. It can be delivered to your own networking group (especially as a second half presentation following the "Networking Safari" format) or at other meetings where they are looking for a 30 minutes standalone presentation.

It is a presentation which is most effective with pictures, appropriate sound effects (there are lots of free, downloadable animal noises available) and music ("The Lion Sleeps Tonight" works well). At various stages I introduced "Birthday Line", "Thanks For The Memory" and various YouTube clips for effect. For each of the following, use one slide, incorporating a picture, a sound and a three-line description of each networking animal's behaviour: -

**White Rabbit**
- Disorganised
- Always the last to arrive
- "Sorry I'm Late"

**Flamingo**
- Arrive with their friends
- Stay with their friends
- Leave with their friends

**Porcupine**
- Stand on their own
- Clam up when approached
- Slow to open up

**Boa Constrictor**

- Really dangerous
- Refuse to let go of you
- Squeeze the life out of you

**Lion**

- Always the predator
- Hunt other attendees
- Can be overpowering

**Kookaburra**

- Over talkative
- Difficult to shut up
- Distracting

**Leopard**

- Can't change their spots
- Not open to new ideas
- Reluctant to change

**Chameleon**

- Always changing
- Inconsistent
- Unpredictable

**Cheetah**

- Fastest of all beasts
- Very quick off the mark
- Difficult to tie down

**Spider**

- Very patient
- Very persistent
- Never give up

## PART 5 (h) – Ten Commandments Of Networking

This presentation should be advertised as "do these ten things and your networking will be successful". It does not apologise for barking out instructions, because all of these actions have been proven to work over many years. Each slide contains one commandment and a few explanatory points.

1. **Do Not Regard It As Selling**

- Not "meet the buyer"
- Not a carefully-selected set of leads
- Not people waiting for your sales pitch
- Networking is a MARKETING activity
- All about relationship building
- Test and Measure, as with other activities

2. **Identify Your Objectives**

- Look at membership of Clubs
- Look at individual networking events
- What are you trying to achieve?
- What will be a good result?
- How will you measure the outcome?

3. **Prepare For Every Event**

- Regard networking as a serious business activity
- Don't "wing it"
- Check time, location, format
- Don't forget the "must take" items

4. **Work The Room Effectively**

- Don't stay with a colleague
- Realise that people are there to meet you

- Ask lots of open questions
- Don't stay too long with one person
- Be seen as a connector of people

**5. Develop A "Memorable" Pitch**

- Speak slowly, clearly & enthusiastically
- Don't try to cover too much ground
- Stress the benefits of what you do
- Give examples of who your customers are
- Make it clear what you are seeking

**6. Write Down Your Takeaways**

- Spend 5 minutes at the end of each event
- Record all the things you will do
- Phone calls, info, invites, research etc
- Incorporate in your "To Do" list

**7. Always Follow Up**

- Previous work is wasted if not followed up
- Deliver your promises without delay
- Takes 4-7 contacts to be recommended
- Phone, e-mail, social media
- Arrange one-to one meetings

**8. Be Patient**

- More than one contact is necessary
- Don't be a nuisance, give folks time
- It can take months for a group to work
- It is marketing, so "drip, drip, drip …"

**9. Be Persistent**

- More than one contact is necessary

- Record the nature & dates of contacts
- Try more than one type of contact
- Remind folks without annoying them
- Indulge in "dignified stalking"

**10. Evaluate Your Networking**

- Networking is a MARKETING activity
- Remember your initial objectives
- Test and measure
- If it is not delivering, change it
- If it is still not delivering, stop it

The final slide is entitled "**Ten Commandments Of Networking**" and lists the "ten" items

1. Do not regard it as selling
2. Identify your objectives
3. Prepare for every event
4. Work the room effectively
5. Develop a "memorable" pitch
6. Write down your takeaways
7. Always follow up
8. Be patient
9. Be persistent
10. Evaluate your networking
11. Always deliver more than you promised

## PART 5 (i) – Three Biggest Mistakes Of Networking

This is a very brief presentation and concentrates on the three most common reasons for networking not to work.

The first slide is entitled **"They Think It Is Selling"** and lists these points

- Only talk about themselves and their products
- Don't listen to anyone else, showing no interest
- Think it is a sort of "meet the buyer" event
- Hunt down potential clients
- Expect instant results
- No orders, so "networking doesn't work"

The second slide is entitled **"They Do Not Prepare"** and lists these points
Check Beforehand

- Venue & Time
- Format
- Other Attendees
- Dress Code
- Cost
- Attendees
- Objectives

"Must Take" Items

- Badge
- Business Cards
- Notes & Prompts
- Pen & Notebook
- Flyers & Leaflets
- Banners
- Diary

The third slide is entitled **"They Fail To Follow Up"** and makes the following points

- Write down your action points
- Get in touch soon
- Do whatever you have promised
- Follow up all leads, be persistent
- Be patient, it is not a "quick fix"
- Maintain a database

The final slide is entitled **"Three Biggest Networking Mistakes"** and summarises those mistakes

1. They think it is SELLING
2. They do not PREPARE
3. They fail to FOLLOW UP

## PART 5 (j) – Working The Room

Networkers do not have long at events to meet lots of people and build relationships. The amount of time for freestyle networking is limited, so it is really important that networkers make use of their time. This presentation looks at the ways in which networkers can put themselves about and get good value.

The first slide is entitled **"Working The Room"** and lists the main questions networkers will ask

- What should I do beforehand?
- What should I do upon arrival?
- How do I approach strangers?
- What are the best ice-breakers?
- How do I get rid of boring folks?
- What do I do at the end?

The next slide is entitled **"Preparation"** and lists these items

Check Beforehand

- Venue & Time
- Format
- Other Attendees
- Dress Code
- Cost
- Attendees
- Objectives

"Must Take" Items

- Badge
- Business Cards
- Notes & Prompts
- Pen & Notebook

- Flyers & Leaflets
- Banners
- Diary

The next slide is entitled **"Arrival"** and lists these items

- Say goodbye to your colleagues at the door
- Clarify the timetable and the format
- Understand badges, table numbers etc
- Scrutinise the delegate list
- Start over at the teas & coffees

The next slide supports your demonstration of how to approach people, entitled **"Approaching Strangers"**

- Singletons
- Closed 2s
- Open 2s
- Open 3s
- Groups

The next slide is entitled **"Ice-Breakers"** and includes this list

- Weather
- First time here?
- Had a good journey?
- Can you introduce me?
- Ask open questions about themselves

The next slide is entitled **"Not A Moment To Lose"** and gives practical tips

- Don't stay with the same people
- Exchange introductions then move
- Get yourself connected

- Avoid being monopolised
  *Visit coffee stand or toilet*
  *Introduce the past tense*
  *Pass them on to someone else*
- Collect cards and record actions

The final slide is entitled **"Takeaway"** and makes these points

- Don't dash off at the end
- Carry on working the room
- Ask the organiser about anyone you have missed
- Write down your action points
- Arrange one-to-one meetings afterwards

# PART 6

# ICE BREAKERS

"When one door of happiness closes, another opens. But often we look so long at the closed door that we do not see the one which has been opened for us." (Helen Keller)

"Problems are only opportunities in work clothes." (Henry Kaiser)

Whenever people commence networking, they say that it is difficult to get started. They are unsure how to approach people and don't know what to say to break the ice. When you are running a networking event, or merely delivering a presentation on networking, it is important therefore to get the attendees talking to each other.

In this part, I have included a few ways in which you can get attendees to come out of their shells and talk to others. Some are just a fun way of starting to mix and others help to demonstrate a particular networking point.

The activities included in this part are: -

- Birthday Line
- Listen 1 and Listen 2
- Present and Back
- Revealing Threesomes
- So What?
- Thanks For The Memory

**Birthday Line**

This exercise is very simple to set up, it is a bit of fun, and it gets people talking. It also demonstrates a significant principle of networking.
Ask all attendees to leave their seats and stand in one long line, facing you. Explain that you don't like disorderly things, so you would like them to stand in the order in which their birthday comes during the year. So give them a couple of minutes to put themselves in order – 1st January at one end and 31st December at the other end. This has nothing to do with ages, just the dates during the year.

When they have finished, get them to call out their birthdays to check that they are all in order. If someone has a birthday on that particular day, maybe give them a bottle of wine or some chocolates. You can then tell the group what they have achieved: -

- They approached people, some of whom would have been strangers
- They asked those people for information
- They did not meet with any hostility

So, they have started the networking process by approaching strangers in a friendly way, and then asked them questions about themselves. The message being – don't approach people and talk all about yourself, instead ask them about themselves.

**Listen 1 and Listen 2**

They say that at networking events you should recognise that you have two ears and one mouth – and you should use them in the same ratio. In other words, listen twice as much as you speak. But there are two ways in which you can listen, and this exercise demonstrates the effectiveness of each.

a. Put the group into pairs, preferably pairing everyone up with someone they don't know very well. They can either present a spoof elevator pitch that you have provided, or they can present their own business.
b. The first person then spends 60 seconds presenting to the second person – who reacts by being the most enthusiastic listener on earth. Lots of eye contact, nodding, encouragement and genuine interest.

c. Then the second person spends 60 seconds presenting to the first person – who reacts by being the least enthusiastic listener on earth. Lots of distracted looks, yawns, phone-checking and little or no eye contact.
d. Each pair is then asked to compare the two experiences and understand how being an enthusiastic listener can actually help fellow networkers – and of course it is the polite thing to do anyway.

**Present And Back**

All networkers are keen to get their messages across and they are very enthusiastic when called upon to deliver. But they can sometimes be less enthusiastic when it is someone else's turn. Also, some networkers deliver pitches which are downright difficult to remember. This exercise addresses both issues.

a. Put the group into pairs, preferably pairing everyone up with someone they don't know very well. They can either present a spoof elevator pitch that you have provided, or they can present their own business.
b. The first person spends 60 seconds presenting to the second person
c. Then you introduce a nasty surprise!
d. The second person also has 60 seconds – but instead of presenting their own pitch, they have to repeat back what the first person has just said!

After the second presentation, you tell them what they have learned from that exercise: -

- The second person knows whether he or she is a good listener

- The first person knows how good a listener the second person is and the second person also knows how easy to remember the pitch was.
- If the pitch wasn't repeated accurately, it may be because the second person is a poor listener – but it may be because the pitch itself is not sufficiently memorable. Or both!

**Revealing Threesomes**

Part of building a strong networking group is helping the participants to understand more about the people, as well as about the businesses. This exercise helps delegates to learn more about each other, in a fun way.

a. Put the group into threes (you may need to ask two people from the same organisation to double up if the numbers do not fit, or you may join one of the groups yourself).
b. The threesomes are given ten minutes to come up with three business facts about the trio – one of which is true and the other two are not true. Each threesome is then invited to stand up and present the three "facts", and the rest of the group will try to identify which one is true.
c. Time permitting, this exercise can be repeated, but using personal facts rather than business facts. This version is usually more raucous – and revealing!

**So What?**

Whenever a networker stands up and presents an elevator pitch to the room, the listeners are only listening out for what is in it for them. They are waiting to understand the benefit of the product or service before them. Surprisingly, it takes some people a while to appreciate what their own actual benefit is. This exercise helps them to focus.

a. Again, put the group into pairs, preferably pairing everyone up with someone they don't know very well. Each delegate presents their own business to the other person, explaining what they supply or do.
b. The other person replies at the end of each sentence with the words "so what?"
c. This continues as long as is necessary until the second person actually gets down to the benefit. (Where a business is supplying a business service, there are basically only 3 possible benefits – increase sales, reduce costs and save time).
d. The actual benefit should then be incorporated very early into future elevator pitches. If the listener is waiting for the benefit, give it to them early.

**Thanks For The Memory**

This is a very powerful way of explaining to networkers how to structure their elevator pitches. It was given to me by an excellent speaker at networking events, Keith Warren, and I managed to sneak it into a number of presentations. It involves showing people a set of words on a Powerpoint presentation, where the slides automatically advance after about 3 or 4 seconds. At the end, the attendees are asked a few questions, the answers to which reveal some interesting facts. Before starting, inform delegates that they must not write anything down nor type into their laptops until the end, as this would defeat the object of the exercise.

- I recommend 30 slides, each containing one word

- The slides should auto advance after 3 or 4 seconds
- One word should be in a different colour
- One word should be a person's name (Elvis, Rembrandt, Lenin, Madonna etc)
- One word should appear three times in total (but not on consecutive slides)

At the end of the slide show, ask the delegates to write down the following: -

1. The first five words they saw
2. The final five words they saw
3. The word which appeared in a different colour
4. The word which was a person's name
5. The word which appeared more than once

Ask for a show of hands when you reveal the answers and then explain what has happened: -

1. Far more people remembered the early words than the late words
2. Almost everybody spotted the word in a different colour
3. Almost everybody spotted which word was someone's name
4. Almost everybody spotted which word was repeated

So, when putting together an elevator pitch: -

- The benefit is the important part, it is what people are waiting to hear – so include it right at the beginning of the pitch (when it will be remembered), not at the end
- Do something visual – a prop, a gesture, something to wear
- Drop the odd name into the pitch – examples of customers you have served

- Repeat the important things, like contact details

Those things will make the pitch more memorable – so other delegates can pass on the message! This exercise makes important points in a very effective way and can be rolled out within a number of different networking formats.

# PART 7

# MAKING ROUNDS OF ELEVATOR PITCHES MORE INTERESTING

“I do not object to people looking at their watches when I am speaking – but I strongly object when they start shaking them to make certain they are still going.” (Lord Birkett)

“Money can’t buy friends, but it can get you a better class of enemy.” (Spike Milligan)

Delivering elevator pitches at networking events is fundamentally important. These are opportunities for businesses to put themselves in the shop window, they are chances to create good impressions and they enable businesses to build lasting business relationships. But, if you use the same old format every time, there is a chance that delegates will get bored and perhaps stop concentrating on other delegates' pitches.

There are a number of ways in which rounds of elevator pitches can be made more interesting. Most of these are very simple to set up and just require the organiser to read the newspapers or search the Internet beforehand. They can be categorised into (a) seasonal, (b) current, (c) historic and (d) procedural.

**(a) Seasonal Themes**

*New Year's Resolution* – at the first event after the turn of the year, ask delegates to end their pitches by sharing a New Year's resolution with the group. This could be a business or a personal resolution and you could also ask them to state what they are going to do to ensure that they stick to it.

*Chinese New Year* – find out which animal is associated with the Chinese New Year just beginning and ask for contributions pertaining to that animal. This could include why the business or owner is like that animal, how the business might perform like that animal over the next year etc.

*Easter Bunny* – at any time during the lead up to Easter, ask delegates to end their pitches by saying what they would like the Easter Bunny to bring for their business, and why. Maybe give a large Easter egg to the best or most imaginative speaker – and small chocolate eggs for everyone else.

*Midsummer Madness* – ask delegates to share a brave, bold, wacky or downright mad idea which they have tried in their business. If they cannot volunteer one of their own, maybe they could just share a mad idea they have seen other businesses employ.

*Scary Halloween* – during October you could mention that the scariest event of the year has arrived, Halloween. Ask delegates to declare what is the scariest thing facing their business at present, and what they are doing to lessen its impact.

*Christmas Fairy* – in a similar vein, at any time during the lead up to Christmas, ask delegates to end their pitches by saying what they would like the Christmas Fairy (or maybe Santa Claus himself) to bring for their business, and why. Maybe give a seasonal goodie to the best or most imaginative speaker.

**(b) Current Themes**

*Glastonbury* – at any time during the music festival season, ask delegates to include in their pitches which band their business is like, and why. Maybe you could give a few examples, complete with sound.

*In The Book* – around the time of the Hay Festival (or similar event), ask delegates to nominate which author or book is like their business, and why. You could also ask delegates to nominate the best business book they have read.

*On Me 'ead Son* – at the time of big sporting events (FIFA World Cup, Ashes test matches, Wimbledon etc) ask delegates to say which sportsman or team is most like their business, and why. Give examples, supported by photographs or video clips.

*Revelations* – at the end of their pitches, delegates must share a secret about themselves with the group. These could be business or personal secrets and maybe a prize could be awarded for the biggest revelation.

*Mother Nature* – whenever there is extreme weather about, some businesses struggle with the unexpected conditions (sports events, outdoor fairs, music festivals etc). Ask delegates to share the type of unforeseen events which could affect their businesses, and how they can manage those risks.

**(c) Historic Themes**

*All You Need Is Love* – around the time of any Beatles anniversaries (birthdays, deaths, release of albums etc) ask delegates to include a Beatles song title somewhere in their pitches. Just be prepared - some bright spark will always just stand up, say "Help", and then sit down again!

*Chickie Run* – around the time of any film-related anniversaries (stars' birthdays, film release dates etc) pick up any themes or scenes from films and get delegates to include something related in their pitches. For instance, in the James Dean film "Rebel Without A Cause", there is a scary sequence called the “Chickie Run”. Delegates are asked to share a scary event for their business, and how they have coped with it.

*Inspirational Figures* – delegates are asked to nominate an historical figure (politician, inventor, writer, composer etc) who has inspired them, and why.

*Gettysburg Address* – this only really works for small groups where time is not tight. Point out that one of the most memorable speeches ever delivered, the famous Gettysburg Address, only took Abraham Lincoln 2 minutes and 20 seconds to deliver. Ask delegates to deliver a business pitch in 2 minutes and 20 seconds.

*Pearl Harbour* – there are many historical events which provide themes to be applied. For instance, the surprise attack on Pearl Harbour can be used as an example of the unexpected. Delegates are asked which events have surprised their businesses, and how they coped with them.

*To Be Or Not To Be* – around the time of Shakespeare’s birthday, ask delegates to incorporate a Shakespearean reference into their pitch. This could be a play title, a character or a quote.

**(d) Procedural Variations**

*And The Winner Is* – after every delegate has pitched, each table is asked to agree which person on their table gave the “best” pitch. This could be the most eloquent, the funniest or even the bravest pitch. The table winners then give another pitch to the room and the one judged to be the best gets a prize.

*Lucky Dip* – many networkers become nervous as their turn to speak draws ever nearer. It has been called "creeping death". A way of overcoming this is for the group leader to call the next speaker from a list of delegates. Maybe this method could be used at every third or fourth meeting just to provide some variety.

*Nominations* – alternatively, after each speaker finishes their pitch, they nominate the next speaker. This is another example of how to inject variety.

*Volunteers* – let the delegates themselves determine the speaking order by asking them to put themselves forward as the next speaker. So it is a question of "right, who wants to go next?"

# PART 8

# TWENTY DIFFERENT NETWORKING FORMATS

"It usually takes me more than three weeks to prepare a good impromptu speech." (Mark Twain)

"How come there is only one Monopolies Commission?" (Anon)

I stated earlier in this book that some very well-established networking groups use the same format, and the same agenda, at all their meetings. There is nothing wrong with this, as their continuing success proves. However, I found as a networker myself that I preferred variety as different formats challenged (and educated) me in different ways. When I therefore started running networking groups myself, I introduced what I believe is the largest range of networking formats anywhere.

Some of these formats are simple to run, but others require a lot of preparation beforehand. People who are not as pedantic as me may find some of these too daunting, but hopefully there will be enough here to inject plenty of variety into any networking group. Some of them are more light-hearted than others, but they all have sound business takeaways.

For each of the 20 formats, I have provided: -
**Overview** – what it is and generally how it runs
**Objectives** – what each delegate should be looking to get out of the meeting
**Announcement** – how to tell the world about the event (email attachment, website text, social media text etc)
**Delegate Briefing** – what to tell delegates prior to the meeting
**Table Host Briefing** – what to tell table hosts (where they are required)
**Method** – how the meeting is run, with suggested timings
**Props, Aids, Special Forms** – what is used to make the meeting run
**Takeaways** – what delegates should take away from the meeting

These are my suggestions, based upon what I have seen working in practice. All of these formats have been used regularly and, in some cases, extensively. All of them have been used in my own clubs and many of them have been run on behalf of other organisations, either at their meetings or at general business events. Of course, other people will run these events in their own way, depending on locality, numbers and the characteristics of each group.

At the end of this section, I have listed a number of alternative titles for these events.

The twenty different networking formats are :-

(i) Acid Test
(ii) Ask Our Geeks
(iii) Boundarylessness
(iv) Bring A Prop
(v) Deck Of Cards
(vi) Flipchart Fiesta
(vii) Getting To Know You
(viii) Hammering Out A Deal
(ix) Knowledge Carousel
(x) Matrix Networking
(xi) Mini Boardroom
(xii) Monopoly Of Wisdom
(xiii) Networking Bingo
(xiv) Networking Safari
(xv) Open And Closed
(xvi) Pair And Share
(xvii) Send Three And Fourpence
(xviii) Spanish Inquisition
(xix) Speaker Event
(xx) Speed Networking

## PART 8 (i) ACID TEST

**Overview**
This is an exercise in which delegates constructively help each other to become easier to recommend. Some networkers do not get as much out of the networking process as they should – but they don't realise what they are doing wrong. They can learn here what they need to change in order for recommendations and referrals to flow. It can be a 60 minute exercise, following a shortened first half, or it could be a 90 minute exercise (maybe 50 minutes before the break and 40 minutes afterwards).

**Objectives**
Delegates should enter this process with two things in mind – (1) to learn whether the way in which they present their businesses is appropriate and (2) to help other delegates become more credible and recommendable.

**Announcement**
This exercise demonstrates the value of openness and collaboration amongst our members. You do a brief presentation of your business to the other delegates on your table, and then ask the other delegates whether they would recommend you to their contacts, clients and friends.
Constructive feedback then flows as the other delegates will comment upon your pitch, your presentation, your demeanour, your uniqueness and your differentiation. As networkers, we rely upon our fellow networkers to refer and endorse us to others – so this exercise highlights quite clearly what more we can do to make ourselves and our businesses easier to pass on.

**Delegate Briefing**

Fundamental to your success as a networker is the effectiveness of your presentation, or "elevator pitch". Once finished, you should be confident that your message has been understood, so everyone in the room will now go and recommend you to their contacts. In this exercise we are going to test just how effective you are by asking others why they wouldn't buy from you, or why they wouldn't recommend you.

There will be 6 or 7 businesses on your table. The idea is that each business in your group has a few minutes to ask and discuss the question "why wouldn't you recommend me?"

The aim is for each business to receive direct input from potential customers (or people putting themselves in the position of potential customers) on what they would find compelling and persuade them to buy.

This is a unique opportunity for each business to get real market research. There may be a few surprises but this is an important way in which we can help each other to improve. If your regular pitches at networking events do not result in any business, this should help you to understand why.

The feedback a business receives might include: -

- Clarity of offering ("I just don't understand what you do")
- Lack of differentiation ("I can't see what makes you stand out from the others")
- Quality ("I don't know how good your service is yet")
- Price ("It is not clear where you are positioned")
- Relationship ("I just don't feel that I know you well enough yet")

- Personal preferences ("you are pushy, arrogant, negative" etc)

The more specific you are, the more constructive it will be. Where individuals do not use the product or service on offer, ask them to identify the features that would encourage them to recommend it to others.

You have 30 seconds to introduce yourself and your products or services. The next few minutes are then used to get the views and perceptions of the rest of the group – do not waste this time by merely extending your initial sales pitch. At the end you need to summarise what has been learned – and, if possible, what will be implemented. All comments should be made, and received, constructively. Our objective is to help other delegates – and certainly not to leave them feeling depressed.

**Table Host Briefing**

You will have 6 or 7 businesses on your table. The idea is that each business in your group has a few minutes to ask and discuss the question "why wouldn't you recommend me" or "why wouldn't you buy from me?" The aim is for each business to receive direct input from potential customers (or people putting themselves in the position of potential customers) on what they would find compelling and persuade them to buy. This is a unique opportunity for each business to get real market research. As time may be a problem, the Table Host goes last – so if you have not been strict, you will miss out!

The feedback a business receives might include: -

- Clarity of offering ("I just don't understand what you do")
- Lack of differentiation ("I can't see what makes you stand out from the others")
- Quality ("I don't know how good your service is yet")

- Price ("It is not clear where you are positioned")
- Relationship ("I just don't feel that I know you well enough yet")
- Personal preferences ("you are pushy, arrogant, negative" etc)

The more specific you can get people to be, the better it will be. Where individuals do not use the product or service on offer, ask them to identify the features that would encourage them to recommend it to others.

Each business has 30 seconds to introduce themselves and their products or services. The next few minutes should be used to get the views and perceptions of the rest of the group – this time should not be used by the business merely justifying or extending the initial sales pitch. This is the most difficult thing for the Table Host to control, so be strict. Everyone should contribute, as all views are valid. All comments should be made, and received, constructively – not to depress each other. Individuals should not be allowed to stray from the subject. At the end of each discussion, allow each business to summarise what has been learned – and, if possible, what will be implemented.

**Method**

This exercise can be one of the most constructive and beneficial tools in a networking leader's armoury, but it takes careful organisation for it to work! You cannot just throw delegates' names into a hat and allocate a random six names per table – then just hope for the best.
Ideally there will be six people per table, allowing ten minutes each, so one hour in total. Allowing fifteen minutes each will work fine, so 90 minutes in total (perhaps wrapped around a break). But, if delegates get

less than ten minutes each, it will be too rushed and delegates will feel cheated.

- Make a list of all delegates and their businesses
- Colour code males and females
- Colour code the business sectors (finance, legal, business support, printers, marketing, healthcare etc)
- Distinguish new members and guests
- Select the table hosts. These are people who are good facilitators, good timekeepers and (if possible) known to the other delegates. The performance of the table hosts will have a significant effect upon the success or otherwise of the activity
- Allocate the other delegates to the tables, separating people from the same sector, ensuring a comfortable gender balance across all tables and spreading the new members and guests across all tables. If possible, any known "strong" characters should be allocated to the more experienced table hosts
- The table plan is so important, but then it has to be changed at the very last minute when you know who has and who hasn't turned up. These late alterations still have to recognise the same principles in order to maintain those balances. You may have to ask two people from the same organisation to act as one person for this exercise.
- Confirm the timings to the table hosts at the start and then remind them when there is ten minutes to go. During the session, you should move around the room, joining the tables in turn, to get a flavour of the sort of things being fed back. At the end of

the exercise, ask delegates to write down three things that they will do differently. You should offer a vote of thanks to the table hosts and invite applause from the delegates

This exercise works just as effectively online as face-to-face. You just need to allocate participants to "rooms" or "tables" in advance of the meeting, to ensure there is no duplication.

**Props, Aids, Special Forms**

The delegates do not need anything special for this exercise. The organiser's all-important table plan is the only thing out of the ordinary.

**Takeaways**

Delegates will either receive reassurance that they are on the right lines, or they will receive constructive ideas on how they can improve. If they implement some or all of those ideas, this exercise can be extremely useful. In addition, delegates will have helped each other and continued to develop ever-closer relationships.

## PART 8 (ii) ASK OUR GEEKS

**Overview**

This is a simple but different format which can be used instead of a standard speaker event, during the second half of the meeting, after all the elevator pitches have been delivered. Typically, it should last for 45 to 60 minutes. It gives the technical experts in the group a chance to show off their expertise, whilst giving other delegates a chance to get those awkward questions answered.

**Objectives**

Delegates should approach the meeting with the intention of getting some answers to their questions, whilst enhancing their knowledge of all things computer and telecoms related.

**Announcement**

The second half of our meeting consists of a panel session using our own internal experts, answering questions on IT, Cloud Computing, Websites, Internet, Telecoms, Social Media, Apps.

So, if you have problems in any or all of these areas, this is the meeting to attend. At this meeting, you will meet the very people in the club who know how to find all the answers to your problems. We don't need to import the expertise, we already have it within the membership, so this is the chance to ask those awkward questions you have been storing up for ages. And we promise the answers will not be in techno jargon!

**Delegate Briefing**

The second half of our meeting consists of a panel session using our own internal experts, answering questions on IT,

Cloud Computing, Websites, Internet, Telecoms, Social Media, Apps.
So, if you have problems in any or all of these areas, you will meet the very people in the club who know how to find all the answers to your problems. We haven't needed to import the expertise, we already have it within the membership, so this is the chance to ask those awkward questions you have been storing up for ages. And we promise the answers will not be in techno jargon!

**Table Host Briefing**
Table hosts are not required for this format.

**Method**
Assemble a group of members who are experts in the IT/Telecoms/Social Media sectors, if possible without too much of an overlap.
As part of the invitations, members and guests will have been asked to submit questions for the panel. But these will probably not be sufficient, so you will need to add more questions yourself. Adding questions yourself enables you to ensure that a good range of topics can be covered, involving all the panellists. You will probably need about 20 questions, as some will lead to supplementary questions during the evening.
Before the meeting, try to group the questions into categories (social media, smart phones, backup etc). Send a list of the questions to the panellists in advance and then encourage the panellists to meet up before the meeting to discuss who is the best-equipped to take the lead on each answer.
During the meeting, ask the questions in an order which ensures each panellist gets the chance to contribute and also take care that one over-enthusiastic panellist doesn't

dominate proceedings. Watch out for supplementary questions before moving on to the next question.
As a thank you to the panellists, make sure that their contact details are circulated to all delegates after the meeting, together with links to any websites which have been mentioned in the answers.

**Props, Aids, Special Forms**
Delegates do not need anything special for this event. The sorted list of questions is needed by the organiser (and the panellists if possible).

**Takeaways**
All delegates should have learned from the experts' answers, irrespective of who submitted the questions. And the individual panellists will have enhanced their reputations amongst the other delegates.

## PART 8 (iii) BOUNDARYLESSNESS

**Overview**

I believe that the term "Boundarylessness" was first used by Jack Welch, the CEO of General Electric, in the early 1990s. He discovered that some of the companies within the large GE group had information and relationships which could help other businesses within the group – if only they knew. So he introduced the principle of "Boundarylessness" to enable his companies to come away from their silos and explore how they could help each other. I took part in a number of these exercises and saw how fruitful they could be, so I applied the principle to members of my local networking club.

This exercise requires absolute openness on the part of the participants and a desire to help one another. Delegates share details of their commercial relationships and then explore how they can use each other's relationships for mutual gain.

**Objectives**

Delegates should enter this meeting with two objectives, (1) to use their knowledge and contacts to help the other delegates and (2) to get help from other delegates in order to get introductions and referrals. Delegates must have a give and take attitude.

**Announcement**

This format can only work with a group of carefully-selected participants. With respect, it is not for accountants, solicitors etc, as it could compromise client confidentiality. It should not be broadcast outside of the invited group.

**Delegate Briefing**

This meeting is only available to a selected group of non-competing delegates, all of whom are open-minded and collaborative. It could be the most fruitful meeting you will attend for some time, although it will involve you in plenty of hard work! You will be asked to open up and share with the group the details of your strongest commercial relationships (suppliers, customers, local authorities, banks, collaborators etc). You will also be asked to declare which target organisations you have (again not necessarily just customers). Other delegates will do the same.

All delegates then creatively work together to establish what matches there are between the respective lists – looking to find who is targeting organisations which are already known to the other delegates.

A list of action points will be circulated to all delegates after the meeting, recognising who is going to do what – and by when. A subsequent follow-up meeting will be arranged within 2 months to check on progress.

**Table Host Briefing**

The organiser of the networking group will normally chair the meeting, although this can be delegated to another member with particularly good facilitative skills.

**Method**

The most important part of this exercise is the selection of the participants. This can work with up to 8 delegates, although I always found that 6 was the ideal number – large enough to generate lots of ideas but not too unwieldy. The participants must be open-minded, creative and generous. Having said that, it must be agreed beforehand that conversations within the group should

stay within the group. In addition to these points, the participants must not be competing with each other – so only one marketing person, only one web designer etc. The process does not work if participants are scared of opening up in front of their rivals.
The first delegate stands up and sticks two flipchart sheets up on the wall. On one sheet they write down between five and ten organisations with which they have strong relationships. On their second sheet they list between five and ten organisations with which they would like contact. The other delegates follow suit and eventually there are a number of pairs of flipchart sheets covering the walls.
The next part of the meeting is the crucial one. All lists of targets are scrutinised to see if they correspond with any of the lists of strong relationships. Similarly, the lists of strong relationships are scrutinised to see what use they can be to the other delegates. Quite a few direct contacts will result, but there will also be some creative indirect routes suggested as well.
The organiser needs to draw up an action list consisting of (1) Organisation to be contacted (2) Person making the introduction (3) Beneficiary and (4) Target date. Other offers of help could have been generated by the session and those should be logged as well.
With the right group of delegates, this session can take at least 2 hours, and perhaps 3 hours. Allow for a break, to keep the delegates fresh. I found that this exercise worked better in the afternoon than in the evening.

**Props, Aids, Special Forms**

The only props needed are flipchart sheets, whatever "sticky" material is permitted by the venue, marker pens and refreshments.

**Takeaways**

The group should take away a large number of action points, especially the chance of being introduced to some key new contacts. They will also know far more about their fellow delegates, which may well lead to future collaboration.

A follow-up meeting should be organised 2 or 3 months afterwards to identify what actions have been taken and what further measures might be necessary to make things happen.

## PART 8 (iv) BRING A PROP

**Overview**
This is one of the simplest formats to organise, one of the simplest to run – but also one of the most fun in which to take part. When networkers merely stand up and deliver their pitches, it can be boring if no-one injects something exciting or different to the proceedings. Networkers should be encouraged to do something visual when delivering their pitches – to catch the eyes of their fellow networkers, make an impression and be memorable.
This exercise gives delegates the chance to be creative and enhance their pitches by using visual props. The delegates still get their normal allotted time for their pitches, but they incorporate the use of their props within their pitches.

**Objectives**
Delegates should go into this exercise with the simple intention of helping other delegates to understand what it is that they do and what the benefits are of their product or service.

**Announcement**
We are always encouraging our delegates to introduce a visual element when delivering their elevator pitches – doing or showing something which will help people to remember their pitches. This could be something to wear, something to demonstrate or something to wave. It needs to be something which helps to get the message across, but without trivialising the business.
At our next meeting we encourage all delegates to "bring a prop" to enhance their elevator pitches and there will be a prize for the prop which most effectively enhances the delegate's pitch – this could be the most dramatic, the

funniest or just the one which best helps to make the message memorable.

**Delegate Briefing**

We are always encouraging our delegates to introduce a visual element when delivering their elevator pitches – doing or showing something which will help people to remember their pitches. This could be something to wear, something to demonstrate or something to wave. It needs to be something which helps to get the message across, but without trivialising the business.

At our next meeting we encourage all delegates to "bring a prop" to enhance their elevator pitches –

- something which has the same characteristics as the business
- something which amplifies a message within the pitch
- something which stresses a strapline
- something which illustrates a logo, brand colour or one of the products being offered

Of course, it is not compulsory to "bring a prop" but there will be a prize for the prop which most effectively enhances the delegate's pitch – this could be the most dramatic, the funniest or just the one which best helps to make the message memorable.

So, time to be creative!

**Table Host Briefing**

No table hosts are necessary for this activity.

**Method**

Whether it be round the room, table by table or completely random, delegates are called upon to deliver their pitches, making effective use of the props they have brought with them. Prizes can be awarded for the most effective and maybe the funniest use of a prop, judged perhaps by a guest speaker or a charity representative.

**Props, Aids, Special Forms**

No special items are required, just the props brought by the delegates.

**Takeaways**

Delegates will have been able to get their messages across more effectively and they will have understood more about the products and services of their fellow participants. In some cases, delegates will continue to use visual aids for all their presentations going forwards.

## PART 8 (v) DECK OF CARDS

**Overview**

This is a different way of getting networkers to have one-to-one meetings with other delegates and maybe start to build new relationships. It uses playing cards to determine who networks with whom.

**Objectives**

Delegates should go into this exercise with the intention of learning more about their fellow networkers.

**Announcement**

We have made this different type of networking event as participative as possible, so there is plenty of hard work for the delegates.

Upon arrival, everyone receives a playing card and will use the card to take part in four separate rounds of networking. The number, colour and suit of your card will determine with whom you network during the session. There will be three different one-to-one networking sessions and one group activity during the meeting – plus a networking take on the old "Deck Of Cards" number. A great chance to make new connections and strengthen relationships.

**Delegate Briefing**

This is a very participative networking format, whereby we use playing cards to determine with whom you network during the session. Upon arrival you will receive a Delegate Sheet and a playing card. You need to keep that playing card with you for the duration, as you are taken through four different rounds of networking.

• The first round is called "Same Suit", as you deliver a 60 seconds pitch to all those delegates whose cards are the same suit as yours
• The second round is called "Same Colour", as you take part in a one-to-one meeting for 15 minutes with the holder of the card which is the same value and same colour as yours – so the person with the Jack of Hearts meets with the person with the Jack of Diamonds etc
• The third round is called "Different Colour", as you take part in a one-to-one meeting for 15 minutes with the holder of the card which is the same value as yours, but a different colour – so the person with the Jack of Hearts meets with the person with either the Jack of Clubs or the Jack of Spades etc
• And then, finally, you will take part in a one-to-one meeting for 15 minutes with absolutely anyone you like whose card is not the same suit as yours. This is the "Wild Card" round

You will be aided with an on-screen agenda during the three one-to-one meetings, to ensure that you get the most out of the session. At the end of the exercise, you will have a far better idea of what everyone does, and you should take away a number of action points.

**Table Host Briefing**

Table hosts are not required for this exercise.

**Method**

You need to arrange the tables so that there is a pair of adjacent tables for each of the 4 suits – or one large table per suit.

Use jumbo-sized playing cards if possible. Issue one playing card to each delegate. (Ensure that colleagues from the same organisations have cards which are of different numbers and different suits). Give out the cards in order (all the 2s, then all the 3s, then all the 4s and so on), to minimise the number of delegates without matches. Delegates sit at the tables corresponding to the suit of their card. The four rounds proceed as follows: -

1. The SAME SUIT Round - each person has 90 seconds to pitch to the rest of their suit group
2. The SAME COLOUR Round - tell people to stand and pair up with the same number and the same colour as themselves (so 2 of Hearts with 2 of Diamonds, 2 of Clubs with 2 of Spades etc). They have 15 minutes for a one-to-one meeting
3. The DIFFERENT COLOUR Round - tell participants to pair up with the same number but different colour as themselves (so it will be 2 of Hearts with either 2 of Clubs or 2 of Spades). They have 15 minutes for a one-to-one meeting
4. The WILD CARD Round - tell participants to pair up with anyone they like of a different suit. Again, they have 15 minutes for a one-to-one meeting

This exercise works perfectly when the number of delegates is divisible by 4. If you have one person over, you should get two people from the same organisation to double up and act as one. If you have 2 people over, they can take part in rounds 1,2 and 4 but not in round 3. If you have 3 people over, you should participate yourself to even up the numbers.

The above activities should take about 65 minutes and can be used to take up one half of a meeting. Alternatively, you could include a tailored "Deck Of Cards" presentation, which will enhance the meeting substantially and will add about 15 or 20 minutes to the proceedings. The history of "Deck Of Cards" should be presented, playing clips of the recordings by Wink Martindale and

Max Boyce and with references to the other artists to have covered the piece. You then present your own group's version of the "Deck Of Cards", with pictures of the cards alongside the thing you claim it represents. The backing track can be downloaded easily enough, to give the presentation more effect. You need to come up with relevant things (humorous if possible) for the Ace, 2,3,4,5,6,7,8,9,10, Jack, Queen, King, 4 Suits, 12 Facecards, 13 Tricks and 52 Cards. This takes time, but it will be well-received.

**Props, Aids, Special Forms**

2 packs (just in case) of jumbo-sized playing cards, I recommend 125mm x 85mm in size.
Audio clips by Wink Martindale and Max Boyce.
Special "Deck Of Cards" audio-visual presentation with a downloaded backing track.

**Takeaways**

Delegates will have had the chance to pitch to a quarter of the room and they will have had meaningful one-to-one meetings with 3 other participants.

## PART 8 (vi) FLIPCHART FIESTA

**Overview**

Some years ago, the excellent business speaker, Geoff Ramm, collared me at an event and cheekily said "hey, Stokesie, you do networking games don't you? Well I saw one back in the North East a couple of weeks ago and I thought you'd like it." Once I had corrected him by stating that I ran professional networking activities, rather than games, he told me all about it.

This is a fast-moving exercise which is designed to marry the wants of some delegates with the products and services of others. It is a kind of "instant connections" activity which normally leads to a high number of follow ups.

**Objectives**

Delegates can expect to pick up new potential clients as well as new potential suppliers.

**Announcement**

Delegates will take part in an exercise which is designed to create instant connections and identify possible opportunities.

Everyone is given a flipchart sheet, divided down the middle. On one side you write down 5 or 6 things you buy and on the other side you write down the products or services you sell. You then walk around everyone else's flipchart sheets adding a sticker which corresponds to your number on the delegate sheet. This indicates that the listed product or service is "worth a conversation".

Everyone takes away their flipchart sheet, and the stickers which indicate the conversations which can now take place. This will be lively!

**Delegate Briefing**

This meeting is very different – and it may result in some instant results for all delegates. It is an exercise where we try to marry up some delegates' wants with other delegates' offers.

You will be given a large sheet of flipchart paper, which has been divided into two halves, called "I BUY" and "I SELL". Each half allows you to list up to 6 items – so 6 products or services which you buy for your business, and 6 products or services which you are able to offer to consumers or to other businesses.

Your flipchart sheet is laid out on a table, alongside everyone else's. Every delegate is then given a sheet of printed labels, bearing the number which corresponds to your name on the Delegate Sheet.

The labels are used to confirm that you have an interest in discussing an item further – they are not firm statements that you want to buy, neither are they firm commitments that you will sell. They are saying "I'd like to discuss".

Delegates go around the room, looking at all the flipchart sheets on the tables. You stick your numbered labels on other people's flipchart sheets, alongside the items which they buy or sell. Of course you can affix your labels to more than one buyer or seller of similar commodities, and if you run out of labels we can supply more.

After about 30 minutes, or when everyone has finished touring the flipchart sheets, delegates take back their sheets (taking care not to lose any labels which have been affixed).

In the days after the meeting, and using the Delegate Sheet from the meeting, delegates contact those people whose numbered labels have been affixed to their flipchart sheet – to discuss mutual opportunities.

**Table Host Briefing**
Table hosts are not required for this activity.

**Method**
Delegates move around at different speeds, but this exercise takes approximately 40-50 seconds per delegate, so if there are 50 participants the exercise should be done after about 40 minutes.
Before the meeting, or during the half-time break (depending upon when you choose to run it), lay out the flipchart sheets – 2 or 3 per table, depending upon the size of the tables. Place one sheet of pre-numbered labels and one marker pen on each sheet.
Get the participants to line up in front of the flipchart which includes the numbered labels corresponding with their number on the delegate list.
If the sheets are not pre-printed, get each delegate to write on their sheets, at the top, their business name and delegate list number. They then draw a vertical line dividing the sheet into two. The left hand side should be headed "I Buy" and the right hand side should be headed "I Sell". They then write up to 6 things under each heading – areas which they would like to discuss.
Delegates then move slowly around the room (without short cuts or omissions) and affix their numbered stickers alongside the relevant item on other people's sheets. This indicates that they would like a conversation – it is not a promise to buy or sell.
When delegates have all arrived back at their own sheets, they check that all stickers on their sheets are secure and they then fold their sheets twice (so they are now A4 size). They then return to their seats.
In the days and weeks after the event, delegates follow up with all the people who added stickers to their sheet.

**Props, Aids, Special Forms**

This a very participative exercise, which requires plenty of space. You might be able to get 2 or possibly 3 flipchart sheets to a table, so divide the expected number of delegates by 2 or 3 to arrive at the number of required tables.

You will either provide pre-printed flipchart sheets or you will provide blank sheets (A2 size), upon which the delegates will write the headings.

You need to provide sheets of labels (preferably yellow, orange or bright green) which are numbered – one complete sheet per delegate. Delegate number 1 on the list picks up a sheet of stickers – all of which bear a number 1. Similarly, delegate number 2 picks up a complete sheet of number 2s – and so on.

Each participant will need a marker pen with which to write on their flipchart sheet.

**Takeaways**

Delegates take away plenty of material with which to make some real connections, and quickly. This can be one of the most instantly effective networking formats of all.

## PART 8 (vii) GETTING TO KNOW YOU

**Overview**

This format is one to be kept in hand for those rare occasions when your speaker fails to show – or maybe when someone asks you at the drop of a hat to arrange something to use up a spare 30 minutes. It is easy to set up, but still gives the delegates something meaningful to take away. It kind of "forces" delegates into one-to-one meetings, which they should be setting up themselves anyway.

**Objectives**

Delegates should be looking to learn about other networkers and to develop closer business relationships.

**Announcement**

The most important element within your networking activity is following up. It is pointless collecting business cards, flyers and delegate lists if you do not grasp the opportunity by arranging one-to-one meetings.
Only by getting to know delegates better can you begin to understand how both parties can help each other. At this meeting, we will demonstrate how deeper one-to-one meetings can greatly open up the number of possibilities for networkers.

**Delegate Briefing**

The most important element within your networking activity is following up. It is pointless collecting business cards, flyers and delegate lists if you do not grasp the opportunity by arranging one-to-one meetings.
Only by getting to know delegates better can you begin to understand how both parties can help each other. This

exercise will demonstrate how deeper one-to-one meetings can greatly open up the number of possibilities for networkers.

You will be asked to pair up with someone who is: -

• not from your table, as you are already familiar with them
• not a colleague
• preferably not someone you already know well

Networking is an element within your marketing activities, it is not selling. Similarly, these one-to-one sessions are not about monopolising someone by pinning them against the wall while you sell at them.

Each pairing has 15 minutes together. Whilst we will indicate when the time is halfway through, it is not important that you formally "change over" at that stage. It is more important that you question each other to understand the following: -

• what do they do – what is their product or service?
• what is unique or different about them?
• what benefits do their customers get?
• who are their customers?
• who or what are they looking for?

At the end of the 15 minutes period, everyone should know: -

1. Enough about the other person to be able to deliver a 30 seconds pitch for them
2. Exactly who or what they are looking for
3. What action you can take away in order to help them (introductions to make, information to send, links to websites or other networking groups etc)

You will then repeat the process with someone else

At the end of the evening you will have got to know 2 businesses in more depth – and you will have taken away some action points which will help those businesses.

Similarly, you can expect to receive some items of help for your business.

**Table Host Briefing**
Table hosts are not required for this format.

**Method**
The first thing to do is to ask the delegates to pair up with someone that they do not know very well. There is nearly always one pair who end up with no-one else to meet other than someone they have known for ages. In that case you need to intervene and arrange a swap with another pairing.
On the screen show them a sort of "agenda" for their one-to-one session: -
Could we present each other's business?
Do we know what each other is seeking?
Have we agreed on how we will help each other?
Remind the delegates when they are halfway through, and again when there are 2 minutes left.
This is repeated one or two more times (so either 30 or 45 minutes for the session in total).

**Props, Aids, Special Forms**
No special props are required for this event.

**Takeaways**
Delegates will have action points with which to help other businesses and they will have learned much about the other delegates. And they might even get some new direct or indirect leads out of the conversations.

## PART 8 (viii) HAMMERING OUT A DEAL

**Overview**

This a highly-participative exercise where delegates learn about negotiating techniques and then demonstrate what they have learned in practical face-to face negotiations. After going through the seven standard stages of a negotiation, the delegates are put into threes (buyer, seller and observer), then the buyer and seller try to do a deal in a situation which is presented to them. The observer makes notes and leads a post-deal review.

**Objectives**

Delegates should enter into this activity prepared to learn some negotiating techniques and to show how skilled they are at doing deals.

**Announcement**

In all aspects of business life we find ourselves negotiating – to achieve sales, to purchase raw materials, to acquire services or to hire employees. But how sound is our technique? Do we respect the same disciplines when buying and selling?

To start the session we will look at the "7 Standard Stages Of A Negotiation" and will identify some clues as to what makes an excellent negotiator. Then you will be placed into threes – a seller, a buyer and an observer, who will work together on a transaction. A 20 minute negotiation takes place between the seller and the buyer, with the objective of hammering out a deal which is acceptable to both parties. Meanwhile the observer makes notes with which to lead the subsequent review.

**Delegate Briefing**

This meeting is very participative, and hopefully you will find it useful for your business as well as being enjoyable. In all aspects of business life we find ourselves negotiating – to achieve a sale, to purchase raw materials, to acquire a service or to hire an employee. But how sound is our technique? Do we respect the same disciplines when buying and selling?
To begin with, we will take a look at the "7 Standard Stages Of A Negotiation" with some clues as to what makes an excellent negotiator.
You will be placed into threes – a seller, a buyer and an observer, who will work together on a transaction. You will receive a general brief which introduces the parties and circumstances in your transaction.
Then you will each be given your individual briefs (seller, buyer and observer) which the other members of your trio cannot see. You then spend a few minutes digesting the brief and planning the negotiation.
A 20 minute negotiation takes place between the seller and the buyer, with the objective of hammering out a deal which is acceptable to both parties. Meanwhile the observer watches the behaviour and makes notes with which to lead the subsequent review.
Finally, the buyer, seller and observer discuss what happened during the negotiation and explore how things might have been handled differently.

**Table Host Briefing**

There is no requirement for table hosts in this exercise.

**Method**

The first part of this exercise involves the running of a Powerpoint presentation taking the attendees through the

seven standard stages of a negotiation. I suggest a series of slides explaining each of these 7 stages: -
Prepare, Open, Clarify, Explore, Bargain, Close, Sustain.

1. **Prepare**
- Know what you want and decide what is important
- Understand their position and any differences between you
- Understand the consequences
2. **Open**
- Put your case forward
- Listen closely to their case
- Understand their issues
- Assess their expectations
3. **Clarify**
- Support your case
- Try to expose their case
- Gather information
- Challenge and discuss
4. **Explore**
- Seek understanding
- Probe possibilities
- List all their requirements
- Observe behaviour & signals
5. **Bargain**
- Assemble potential trades
- Make bids
- Compare your cost and their value
- Seek rewards for every concession
6. **Close**
- Build commitment to the items already traded & agreed
- Confirm both are happy with the outcome
- Reach final agreement

7. **Sustain**

- Ensure what has been agreed actually happens
- Re-open the deal if flaws need to be eliminated

*Those points can be consolidated by adding a couple more slides, as follows:-*

**7 Ways To Negotiate Effectively**

- Learn to flinch – even look shocked
- Recognise that people ask for more than they expect
- Be aware that the party with most information performs better
- Be persistent without being demanding
- Try not to "go first" on prices
- Know when to shut up
- Maintain your walk away point

**Characteristics Of Good Negotiators**

- They are patient
- They have a "win/win" mindset
- They are creative
- They are flexible
- They ask lots of questions
- They control their emotions
- They summarise regularly

Tips should be given as to what makes a successful negotiation – and maybe a few things NOT to do.

Divide the room into groups of three and issue each group with the General Briefs – either hand them out or ask them to choose which one they want. It makes sense not to have two adjacent groups working on the same scenario, so you may have to move some folks.

Each trio reads its General Brief and then agrees on the roles, so who will be the Seller, who will be the Buyer and who will be the Observer. Do not force anyone to take on any of the roles – if anyone is less than happy, see if you can get them to swap with someone else.

The Seller and Buyer then have about 20 minutes to do a deal – if possible. Meanwhile, the Observer leads the review after the deal has been struck. As time goes on, some trios will finish early and some will need threatening with a deadline. Try to give them time to conclude if you can.

There are no right and wrong outcomes. If the Seller and Buyer are both happy with the deal, it matters not that another Buyer in a different group got a lower price. It should be pointed out that, if some people have held out for so long that a deal has not been done, that in itself is not a successful result.

This exercise works best if the number of delegates is divisible by 3. If you have one person over, have 2 observers in one of the groups, if you have two people over, run one of the groups without an observer.

**Props, Aids, Special Forms**

There is an awful lot of preparatory work required for this exercise, though once it has been set up you can merely re-print for future sessions. You do not have to invent new networking scenarios every time.

Try to make at least 4 and preferably 6 different negotiations available. These should be varied – for instance (i) secondhand sports car, (ii) printer cartridges, (iii) foreign language courses, (iv) managed office accommodation, (v) services of an interim finance director and (vi) social media services. For each negotiating scenario, you need to produce a General Brief, a Seller's Brief, a Buyer's Brief and an Observer's Brief. The last three Briefs include the General Brief plus the individual pieces of information that the other parties cannot see. Here is an example of a negotiating scenario involving a secondhand car: -

*GENERAL BRIEF*

*The seller advertised a secondhand Jaguar sports car online and after initial telephone contact the buyer has arrived in Devon to discuss a possible purchase.*

*Jaguar XK8 V8 Coupe 4.0 litre (automatic) Petrol 2 door (reg 1998) 160,000 miles, private plate M40 LTR*

*Racing Green, outstanding spec and condition, cream leather interior, 5 seats, alloy wheels*

*Just passed MOT, rear tyres low on tread, full detailed service history and bills are available for inspection*

*Online Advertised Price £3,995*

*The buyer has travelled from Bristol, has just test-driven the car, and likes it*

*SELLER'S BRIEF*

*Delivery to the buyer's address in Bristol will cost £150 for the seller to arrange*

*Servicing by the seller's friend will only cost £200, but is worth £350 to a potential buyer*

*It will cost £100 to valet the car*

*The seller has a spare, brand new Sat Nav which retails online at £200*

*1 year membership of the Jaguar Owners Club is worth £100*

*The seller has not included a warranty but could include 3 months for £250*

*The seller is keen to sell soon, as cash is needed before the weekend to put a £2500 deposit on a secondhand "dream" car*

*Bottom line for the seller is £3400 in cash, at least £2500 of which is needed this week*

*BUYER'S BRIEF*

*The buyer lives during the week at Bristol but plans to use the car at the family home in Derby*

*The buyer has owned several Jaguar models in the past and has attended Jaguar events*

*The buyer's brother has a fleet of trucks and can collect the car to save on delivery charges*

*The car is due for a service in 2 months – the buyer would like the seller to pay for this*

*The buyer is not technical, so would like a 12 months warranty ideally*

*The buyer would like 1 year AA membership, worth £150 (no use at fixing problems)*

*The buyer doesn't have a sat nav but realises that it would be useful*

*The buyer doesn't need the car for 2 weeks but could take it earlier – although the brother cannot go to collect it for 10 days*

*The buyer had planned to spend £3300 on a new car, plus £300 for sat nav and AA subs*

*The buyer only has £2700 in cash, but expects an insurance cheque for £2000 next week*

*OBSERVER'S BRIEF – make notes about the parties' performances*

*Open* *were they clear, did they give away too much, were they concise?*

*Clarify* *did they question, did they challenge and probe?*

*Explore* *were they creative, did they genuinely try to find a way?*
*Package* *did they concede too much, were they inflexible, were they weak?*
*Close* *did they seek a win-win, was there absolute clarity and agreement?*
*Specifically: -*

- *at what stage did they open up with their "hidden" information?*
- *when the seller had something extra to offer, what was asked for?*
- *if the buyer made life easier for the seller, was a concession requested?*
- *how did they react to surprises?*
- *did they end up with a sensible, sustainable deal?*

**Takeaways**

In an enjoyable atmosphere, delegates will take away a better understanding of the negotiating process, as well as learning how good they are at securing a deal.

## PART 8 (ix) KNOWLEDGE CAROUSEL

**Overview**
A number of networking groups have seen the sense in moving delegates around the room, to help them to understand more about other delegates and what they do. In this exercise, most of the delegates stay where they are on their tables – the only people to move are “experts” who conduct a series of 15 or 20 minute clinics for each table in turn.

**Objectives**
This exercise will enable the general delegates to ask burning questions on a number of business-related topics and it also enables the experts to raise their profile, whilst demonstrating their expertise.

**Announcement**
This is an opportunity to pick the brains of some of our members who are experts in their chosen fields. It is a great chance to understand the range of expertise available to us from within the membership. Delegates are spread amongst a number of tables, each of which includes one of our specialists who will field questions from the table on their subject. After 15-20 minutes, the specialists move to different tables – and so on until they have visited all the tables. The specialists have to work very hard during the evening, everyone else gets some high-quality free advice – and there will be opportunities for networking too.

**Delegate Briefing**
One of the keys to effective membership of a networking group is understanding the expertise and support which is

available from other members. Most small business owners find networking groups attractive because they provide access to specialists and the networking culture includes helping each other. At this meeting you get a wonderful chance to experience at first hand the variety of expertise which exists within the group. You will meet a number of specialists, each of them experts in their field, and you will get a taster of the kind of problems they can advise on.

You will be on a table with 6 or 7 other businesses – and the evening starts by introducing yourself to the others on your table for 60 seconds. You will then spend the rest of the event questioning our experts. Each of our specialists will spend 15-20 minutes per table and the idea is that they will receive a number of questions from the delegates – hopefully one each if there is time. These should be relatively straightforward questions which will tease snippets of advice from our experts, without monopolising the session. The objective is for the delegates to get a clear idea of the kind of issues which each expert can address, and hopefully get some real advice on real issues in the meantime. After 15-20 minutes, the delegates remain at their tables – and the specialists move. During the exercise every specialist will sit at all of the tables.

Not every delegate will have an immediate interest in every specialist's area of expertise. Even so, please allow the other delegates to cover all of their points and make notes of any points of interest for your clients or staff. In some cases, there will be people at the table who are also specialists in a particular expert's field. When this happens, it is important not to try and "catch out" our nominated expert, but instead to support and amplify the message being put across. At the end of the event, you will have a better idea of the calibre of member within the group and you will know where to go for advice should you need it. There will be plenty of movement – a real masterclass merry-go-round.

**Specialist Briefing**

Thank you for agreeing to be one of our mobile experts, as we demonstrate to the members what an impressive and varied range of specialists we have in the group.

The members will meet a number of specialists, each of you experts in your field, and they will get a taster of the kind of problems you can advise on. There are to be no prepared presentations as such, the agenda is very much set by the questions asked by the members. It would, however, make sense for you to keep a basic "crib sheet" in case the questions dry up. Initially you will be on a table with 6 or 7 other businesses – and the evening starts by everyone introducing yourselves to the others on your table for 60 seconds. You stay at this table for the first round.

Each of our specialists will spend 15-20 minutes with each of the tables and the idea is that you will receive a number of questions from the delegates – try to ensure that each person on the table gets to ask at least one question if there is time. Avoid giving long drawn-out answers, take such issues off-line if you can. Try instead to give them little snippets of advice - so that the delegates get an idea of the kind of issues which you can address.

After 15-20 minutes, the delegates remain at their tables – and you move. During the exercise every specialist will sit at each of the tables, following the route A, B, C etc. As you sit at each table, please introduce yourself and pass your business cards around the table. Record the names of

any delegates requiring follow up contact, then do so as soon after the meeting as possible.
In some cases, there will be people at the table who are also specialists in your field. When this happens, try to avoid any banana skins which are thrown your way – concentrate instead on seeking agreement from your fellow experts. Don't worry, any attempted "smart alecs" will be seen for what they are by the other delegates. The objective of the evening is for members to get a better idea of the calibre of member within the group and where to go for advice should they need it. This will be a hectic piece of work for you and we appreciate your support.
Hopefully you will gain some customers, or at least some advocates, from the event.

**Method**
Beforehand, you need to estimate the total number of meeting attendees, therefore the number of tables, and then the number of specialists you will need. Try to get no fewer than 5 "non specialist" delegates and no more than 8 per table. So, if you expect 40 in total, that could be 5 tables of 7, plus the 5 specialists. Once you have this information you can calculate how many minutes each specialist will spend at each table – no less than 15 minutes but no longer than 25.
Try to choose specialists from a variety of business sectors, with no overlaps. These could be financial advice, IT support, printing, social media, legal etc. Try also to include at least a couple of relatively new members of the group, as it gives them a chance to establish themselves.
Do not pressure any specialists to take part, they must feel comfortable about it.
All delegates get 60 seconds each to introduce themselves to the other people on their tables. After this, the experts'

clinics take place, with the experts moving on to their next table promptly. Try to wander around the tables, to ensure that the specialists are not just delivering 15 minute sales pitches – they must let the delegates drive the agenda. This exercise works just as effectively online as face-to-face. You just need to manually allocate the specialists to different "rooms" or "tables" whilst leaving the other participants where they are.

**Props, Aids, Special Forms**

Draw up a one page list of the specialists, with their contact details and fields of expertise (plus photo and business logo if you can), and issue this with the delegate lists at the start of the event.

**Takeaways**

The regular delegates will have had the opportunity to ask questions of experts and they should have a much better idea of what each specialist does. The specialists will have raised the profile of their businesses and hopefully established themselves as experts in their field.

# PART 8 (x) MATRIX NETWORKING

**Overview**
This is one of the most hectic, inspiring and effective networking formats around. Delegates are given their own individual routes around the tables to ensure that every delegate meets every other delegate, somewhere, just once. *This format only works with prime numbers*, so 5 tables of 5, 7 tables of 7, 11 tables of 11 and so on.

**Objectives**
Delegates get the chance to meet every other person in the room, so they should go away with a really good number of potential follow-ups.

**Announcement**
This is a really popular structured table networking extravaganza. You will present your business to a table full of other businesses and receive presentations from the others in turn. You will then move around the room, from table to table, presenting your business a number of times to different people each time. Use of a carefully calculated route around the tables ensures that you will meet every single person somewhere during the session – once!
You will need plenty of business cards for this event – and plenty of stamina.

**Delegate Briefing**
This is a frantic table-hopping exercise in which each attendee gets to meet every other business in the room. The success of the evening depends upon how well each attendee observes a few simple rules and courtesies: -

- Everyone has their own unique route around the tables

- Most delegates end up on a different table after each move
- There are a number of businesses per table – but this number may vary
- Each move lasts long enough for each person to have 60 seconds to present to the rest of the table
- Business cards should be passed around the table while the person is presenting
- The time can be used for a presentation, questions etc – but strictly no more than the allotted time of 60 seconds for each person
- We will signify when it is time for the next speaker
- It is important that the next person starts as soon as the previous person ceases
- As soon as the round ends, everyone should proceed swiftly to their next table
- If anyone has lost their "route map" – we have a control sheet, so don't guess!
- Glasses, cups, plates etc should not be left behind – take them, or put them on the side
- The next round starts when all delegates are at their new table

**Table Host Briefing**

This is a frantic table-hopping exercise in which each attendee gets to meet every other business in the room. The success of the evening can depend upon how well the Table Hosts keep to the procedures: -

- Everyone has their own unique route around the tables
- The Table Host only moves tables on the final move
- Everyone else ends up on a different table after each move

- Normally there are 5 or 6 businesses per table – but sometimes as many as 8
- Each person has 60 seconds to speak. We will signify when it is time to move on to the next speaker
- Start with the person to the left of the Table Host and go round clockwise
- Business cards should be passed around the table while the person is presenting
- The time can be used for a presentation, questions etc – but strictly no more than the allotted time of 60 seconds for each person
- It is important that the next person starts as soon as the previous person ceases
- If there is time over at the end, the Table Host decides how best to use it
- At the end of each round, everyone except the Table Host should proceed swiftly to their next table
- If anyone has lost their "route map" – we have a control sheet, there should be no guesses
- Documents, glasses, cups, plates etc should not be left behind
- The next round starts when all delegates are at their new tables
- Table A will contain every Table Host on the final move

**Method**

Print off enough sheets containing the routes around the tables and use a highlighter to denote the attendee's unique route on the chart. If you are using the 7 x 7 format you will need 49 sheets, but print a few extra just in case more turn up and then you can “double up”. Highlight each of the participants until a different route on every sheet has been highlighted. To balance the tables, don’t just give out the sheets in numerical order, issue the table hosts first (1, 8, 15, 22, 29, 36, 43) then the table hosts’ numbers plus one (2,9, 16, 23, 30, 37, 44) then the table hosts’ numbers plus two (3, 10, 17, 24, 31, 38, 45) and so on.

If less than the maximum number turn up, it just means that there will be less people on one of the tables during the final round. If more than the maximum number turn up you can either (a) ask two people from the same organisation to go around as one person or (b) create extra numbers (50, 51, 52 etc) but take care to avoid having too many people on tables B and C on the final round.

Print A4 table cards on which the letter of the table is clearly visible. Use card or table card holders (menu holders).

Read out the house rules before the start and encourage everyone to hand out business cards while they are speaking. It helps if you can call out when each speaker has ten seconds left. It is important that you move people on swiftly after each round, and don’t let them leave their “debris” behind. Watch out for “lost” participants, as there is nearly always one person who mislays or mis-reads their sheet.

If there are 8 rounds and each round takes 7 minutes, that makes 56 minutes, plus 2 minutes in between each round – so 70 minutes in total. You may wish to include a 10 minutes break halfway through, if only for water!

**Props, Aids, Special Forms**

The matrix of routes is of fundamental importance here, so I have included a picture of what the form should look like. Here are (a) the 5 x 5 matrix, (b) the 7 x 7 matrix and (c) a suggested overflow plan for the 7 x 7 matrix. Lines in grey are the Table Hosts, who only move for the final round.

| Delegate | TABLE CIRCULATION PLAN | | | | | |
|---|---|---|---|---|---|---|
| | Move 1 | Move 2 | Move 3 | Move 4 | Move 5 | Move 6 |
| 1 | A | A | A | A | A | A |
| 2 | A | B | C | D | E | B |
| 3 | A | C | E | B | D | C |
| 4 | A | D | B | E | C | D |
| 5 | A | E | D | C | B | E |
| 6 | B | B | B | B | B | A |
| 7 | B | C | D | E | A | B |
| 8 | B | D | A | C | E | C |
| 9 | B | E | C | A | D | D |
| 10 | B | A | E | D | C | E |
| 11 | C | C | C | C | C | A |
| 12 | C | D | E | A | B | B |
| 13 | C | E | B | D | A | C |
| 14 | C | A | D | B | E | D |
| 15 | C | B | A | E | D | E |
| 16 | D | D | D | D | D | A |
| 17 | D | E | A | B | C | B |
| 18 | D | A | C | E | B | C |
| 19 | D | B | E | C | A | D |
| 20 | D | C | B | A | E | E |
| 21 | E | E | E | E | E | A |
| 22 | E | A | B | C | D | B |
| 23 | E | B | D | A | C | C |
| 24 | E | C | A | D | B | D |
| 25 | E | D | C | B | A | E |

| Delegate | TABLE CIRCULATION PLAN | | | | | | | |
|---|---|---|---|---|---|---|---|---|
| | Move 1 | Move 2 | Move 3 | Move 4 | Move 5 | Move 6 | Move 7 | Move 8 |
| **1** | A | A | A | A | A | A | A | A |
| **2** | A | B | C | D | E | F | G | B |
| **3** | A | C | E | G | B | D | F | C |
| **4** | A | D | G | C | F | B | E | D |
| **5** | A | E | B | F | C | G | D | E |
| **6** | A | F | D | B | G | E | C | F |
| **7** | A | G | F | E | D | C | B | G |
| **8** | B | B | B | B | B | B | B | A |
| **9** | B | C | D | E | F | G | A | B |
| **10** | B | D | F | A | C | E | G | C |
| **11** | B | E | A | D | G | C | F | D |
| **12** | B | F | C | G | D | A | E | E |
| **13** | B | G | E | C | A | F | D | F |
| **14** | B | A | G | F | E | D | C | G |
| **15** | C | C | C | C | C | C | C | A |
| **16** | C | D | E | F | G | A | B | B |
| **17** | C | E | G | B | D | F | A | C |
| **18** | C | F | B | E | A | D | G | D |
| **19** | C | G | D | A | E | B | F | E |
| **20** | C | A | F | D | B | G | E | F |
| **21** | C | B | A | G | F | E | D | G |
| **22** | D | D | D | D | D | D | D | A |
| **23** | D | E | F | G | A | B | C | B |
| **24** | D | F | A | C | E | G | B | C |
| **25** | D | G | C | F | B | E | A | D |
| **26** | D | A | E | B | F | C | G | E |
| **27** | D | B | G | E | C | A | F | F |
| **28** | D | C | B | A | G | F | E | G |
| **29** | E | E | E | E | E | E | E | A |
| **30** | E | F | G | A | B | C | D | B |
| **31** | E | G | B | D | F | A | C | C |
| **32** | E | A | D | G | C | F | B | D |
| **33** | E | B | F | C | G | D | A | E |
| **34** | E | C | A | F | D | B | G | F |
| **35** | E | D | C | B | A | G | F | G |
| **36** | F | F | F | F | F | F | F | A |
| **37** | F | G | A | B | C | D | E | B |
| **38** | F | A | C | E | G | B | D | C |
| **39** | F | B | E | A | D | G | C | D |
| **40** | F | C | G | D | A | E | B | E |
| **41** | F | D | B | G | E | C | A | F |
| **42** | F | E | D | C | B | A | G | G |
| **43** | G | G | G | G | G | G | G | A |
| **44** | G | A | B | C | D | E | F | B |
| **45** | G | B | D | F | A | C | E | C |
| **46** | G | C | F | B | E | A | D | D |
| **47** | G | D | A | E | B | F | C | E |
| **48** | G | E | C | A | F | D | B | F |
| **49** | G | F | E | D | C | B | A | G |

| Delegate | TABLE CIRCULATION PLAN | | | | | | | |
|---|---|---|---|---|---|---|---|---|
| | Move 1 | Move 2 | Move 3 | Move 4 | Move 5 | Move 6 | Move 7 | Move 8 |
| **50** | A | B | C | D | E | F | G | B |
| **51** | B | D | F | A | C | E | G | C |
| **52** | C | D | E | F | G | A | B | B |
| **53** | D | G | C | F | B | E | A | D |
| **54** | E | A | D | G | C | F | B | D |
| **55** | A | C | E | G | B | D | F | C |
| **56** | B | C | D | E | F | G | A | B |
| **57** | D | A | E | B | F | C | G | E |
| **58** | E | B | F | C | G | D | A | E |
| **59** | G | E | C | A | F | D | B | F |
| **60** | B | E | A | D | G | C | F | D |
| **61** | C | A | F | D | B | G | E | F |
| **62** | G | B | D | F | A | C | E | C |
| **Wildcard 1** | A | G | A | E | E | B | C | G |
| **Wildcard 2** | F | F | G | C | D | A | D | G |
| **Wildcard 3** | F | C | B | B | A | E | C | F |

### Takeaways

Delegates may well be exhausted after this exercise, but they will have engaged with every person in the room and they will take away lots of potential leads to follow up. The session always creates a buzz in the room and delegates will linger afterwards to carry on networking.

## SIMPLIFIED VERSIONS

### *Simple Rotation*

This is a method of ensuring that during a simple 2-move event the delegates don't meet the same people twice. It is very simple to administer with no preparation required, apart from the printing of table letters on A4 cards.

1. Balance the tables so that nearly every table has the same number of people. And the number of people on each table should be as close as possible to the number of tables – 6 tables of 6, 9 tables of 9 etc.

2. Get the participants to deliver their elevator pitches to the other folks on their table and pass round their business cards.
3. One person should be nominated or elected as the table host – and that person stays at the same table.
4. The person immediately to the left of the table host moves to the next table letter in sequence (so the person to the left of the table host on table C moves from table C to table D). The next person along goes to the table after that (table C to table E) and so on.
5. They move to their second tables and deliver their elevator pitches for a second time – to new people.

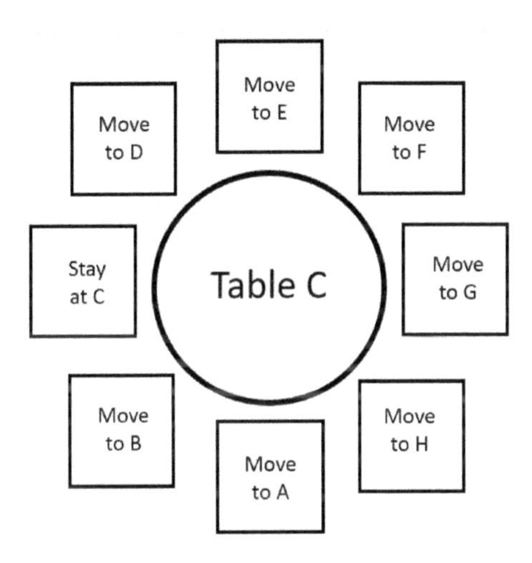


***A + B + Pass***

This a 3-table shuffle which is easy to administer and works irrespective of the number of people taking part. The only preparation is to print table letters on A4 cards and small movement cards (maybe 5cm x 2cm) before the meeting. The small cards will include two letters (preferably in two different colours to ease explanation). If you have 8 tables of 8 for instance, you need to print cards bearing the letters AA, AB, AC, AD, AE, AF, AG, AH, BA, BB, BC etc

1. Balance the tables so that nearly every table has the same number of people. And the number of people on each table should be as close as possible to the number of tables – 6 tables of 6, 9 tables of 9 etc.
2. Get the participants to deliver their elevator pitches to the other folks on their table and pass round their business cards.
3. Give everyone a small card containing two letters – the first letter (on the left of their small card) is the table they are at, the second letter (on the right of their small card) is the table to which they will move. So on table A, one person gets A + A, another person gets A + B, then A + C. On table B, one person gets B + A, another person gets B + B and so on.
4. Get the delegates to move to their second tables – taking their small cards with them.
5. They deliver their elevator pitches for a second time.
6. They then pass their small cards to the people on their immediate left (thus ensuring that they don't all go back to their original tables).
7. They move to their third tables (corresponding to the left of their new small card) and deliver their elevator pitches for a third time – to new people.

## PART 8 (xi) MINI BOARDROOM

**Overview**
In all my years of business networking, this exercise was probably the most valued by the delegates. It enables delegates to benefit from the experience and creativity within the group. Each delegate identifies where they need help. Ideas and constructive suggestions are then fed back to them.

**Objectives**
Delegates need to enter this process with an open mind, prepared to absorb everything which is given to them. They should walk away with real action points with which to tackle their issues.

**Announcement**
This exercise, more than any other, demonstrates the value of openness and collaboration amongst our members.
You do a brief presentation of your business to the other delegates on your table, followed by the identification of a couple of current problems, challenges or concerns you have. Everyone else then works on your business for a quarter of an hour – putting forward suggestions, recommendations, offers of help etc.
At the end, you are asked to summarise and identify a couple of real action points you will take away. And then you get to brainstorm other people's issues. And you will get out of the exercise as much as you put into it ....

**Delegate Briefing**
This exercise is all about business people sharing their business awareness. During the session you will have the opportunity to: –

- Gain new ideas for your business
- Discover new ways to develop your business
- Address some specific business challenges

We will help each other to achieve this by: –

- Thinking 'outside the box'
- Taking part in creative group brainstorming exercises
- Sharing successes – and possible limitations
- Developing mini action plans for each other

You will be working in a focus group of about 6 businesses with a table host (chairperson). Your group will spend approximately 20 minutes 'working' on your business.

- You get 2-3 minutes to briefly present your business and to identify one or two current challenges
- The rest of your table then takes 15 minutes brainstorming, finding solutions and creating ideas for your business
  It is important that you use these 15 minutes to capture all the suggestions being made
- Don't dismiss ideas out of hand and don't use the time just to continue your sales pitch
- You then get 2-3 minutes summarising and deciding which of the suggestions you will take forward

For you to get the most out of your session you will need to introduce your business to the group in a concise manner. You also need to be open about the issues on which you would like help. These might include: -

- I need to improve my social media presence
- I can't get an introduction to a specific buyer at ABC Ltd

- I need to increase my business profile in the XYZ sector
- I need help to refresh my sales literature
- I feel vulnerable because too much of my business is with two large customers
- I need to recruit, but I don't know where to start

Please remember there are no 'Magic Wands' but being open and creative will ensure that you find this session really constructive. Being realistic, the more experienced amongst you will find that you may contribute more than you take away – but this will only make the group stronger.

**Table Host Briefing**

Thank you for agreeing to chair a table at our event. The effectiveness of the Table Host will greatly influence the outcome of the evening for the other people. You will be chairing a group of about 6 business people. The aim is to help them to visualise the potential for their business – to help them 'think outside of the box'.

Each member of your group is to be allocated up to 20 minutes, split like this: -

3 minutes introduction to the group and identification of their "problems"

15 minutes for the group to brainstorm their "problems"

2 minutes to summarise and document their action plan

It's important to try and get all the members of your group to contribute ideas and views to each other. Some may be less outspoken, so please help them to get involved. Try to discourage each participant from merely extending their sales pitch during the 15 minutes brainstorm session – instead they must try to capture all the ideas being thrown at them. Also, no ideas should be rejected out of hand –

they might just work and of course if ideas are consistently bounced back the group will stop making suggestions. After each person has had their time, you should summarise with them to ensure they've been able to make notes of all suggestions and start to build an action plan. There should be a little time at the end for feedback and discussion. It would be helpful if you could share with the room a couple of good examples from your table of how we've assisted each other (as long as the businesses themselves are happy to do so).

**Method**

Delegates at these meetings sometimes think that they were lucky to get on a good table, or that they just happened to get a good table host. Luck does not come into it – the meticulous planning before this meeting is what makes it so successful. The mix of delegates and the choice of table hosts ensures a successful outcome.

- First of all, decide how many delegates are likely to attend and work out how many tables that should involve (allow maybe 7 or 8 per table to allow for no-shows)
- Choose the required number of table hosts – experienced facilitators with well-established businesses who can ensure that all delegates participate
- Then create a list of all the delegates and colour-code them into various sectors (financial, marketing, legal & regulatory, IT, printing etc). Further colour-code them by gender and finally indicate those delegates who are new to the group
- Allocate delegates to tables and ensure that: -

1. Colleagues from the same organisation are kept apart
2. People operating in the same sector (especially obvious competitors) are kept apart
3. There is an even gender balance across the tables
4. There is an even balance of new members and guests across the tables

- When delegates check-in, they are told at that stage which table they are on
- Five minutes before the event starts, you will know which delegates have shown up unexpectedly and which delegates have failed to show. You then have to juggle the tables, whilst still maintaining the sector/gender/new members balance
- During the meeting, you should wander around the tables to understand what kinds of issues are being raised and you can also check the suitability of the table hosts you selected
- Remind the table hosts when there is ten minutes to go. Try and allow enough time for feedback from the table hosts at the end of the session

This exercise works just as effectively online as face-to-face. You just need to allocate participants to "rooms" or "tables" in advance of the meeting, to ensure there is no duplication.

**Props, Aids, Special Forms**

The all-important thing here is the table plan, colour-coded and with enough space for you to write your changes just before the start. No other special items are needed.

**Takeaways**

Delegates should go away with a realistic action plan, which they should incorporate in their "To Do" list. They have also learned a lot more about the businesses of the delegates with whom they shared a table. Some collaborations will probably take place as a result of this meeting.

## PART 8 (xii) MONOPOLY OF WISDOM

**Overview**

This activity is one of the easiest to set up and one of the easiest to run – but for the delegates it can be one of the most beneficial of all the different networking formats. It involves participants opening up and sharing the business lessons they have learned. I once had a boss who told me that no-one has a monopoly of wisdom and this exercise sets out to prove that is the case.

**Objectives**

Delegates must be prepared to open up and, in some cases, admit they have made mistakes. If they do so, they can expect to walk away with some really good advice, based upon other business owners' experiences.

**Announcement**

This is an opportunity to share experiences and learn from each other. Delegates will be given five minutes to consider their answers to a question. Each delegate will then have five minutes to share their answers with the rest of their table – and field any comments or reactions from their colleagues. At the end of the session, the table hosts will share some of their group's answers with the rest of the room.

We will not reveal in advance what question you will have to answer, as we don't want to lose the spontaneity factor. Delegates will learn from the knowledge of the other delegates …. thus preventing a monopoly of course.

**Delegate Briefing**

This networking session is a collaborative, table-based exercise which enables us to share our knowledge and

experience. Running a business can often be a lonely affair, so it is important that we open up, compare experiences and learn from each other. This exercise will enable us to share our knowledge and help each other. After all, no-one has a monopoly of wisdom!
You will be on a table with between 5 and 7 people. Delegates will be challenged with a question, which will relate to your recent business experiences. You will be given 5 minutes to consider your answer(s) to your question and make notes. Every delegate will then have 5 minutes to share their answers with the rest of their table and field comments or reactions from the other delegates. At the end of the session the table hosts present a summary of their tables' answers to the rest of the room. This will be an enlightening demonstration of the range of knowledge and knowhow in the group.

**Table Host Briefing**
This is a collaborative, table-based exercise which enables us to share our knowledge and experience. Running a business can often be a lonely affair, so it is important that we open up, compare experiences and learn from each other. This exercise will enable us to share our knowledge and help each other. After all, no-one has a monopoly of wisdom! You will chair a table with between 5 and 7 people, to make sure everyone gets involved, to keep everything on time, and to present to the room at the end. You will give each delegate a question from an envelope. Delegates will be challenged with a question, which will relate to recent business experiences. If a delegate is uncomfortable with their question, they can exchange with someone else. Everyone is then given 5 minutes to consider their answer(s) to their questions and make notes.

Every delegate will then have 5 minutes to share their answers with the rest of the table and field comments or reactions from the other delegates. Please ensure that everyone gets their fair allocation of time, that everyone takes part, that no-one dominates the responses, and that it is clear what lessons or outcomes have come out of the exercise.
At the end of the session you will present a brief summary of your table's answers to the rest of the room.

**Method**
Each table host is given an envelope, each of which includes 8 individual sheets. Each sheet contains one question to be considered and a few suggestions as to what they might offer as the answers. Before starting the proceedings, just check that everyone is comfortable with their questions – if not, their table hosts can facilitate a swap with other delegates.
I have suggested that after an initial 5 minutes' thinking time each delegate can have 5 minutes to present their answers to their table. Depending upon how many people there are on each table, and also upon how much time you have left in the meeting, this 5 minute allocation can be increased.
You could insist that one person on each table answers question 7, and then ask each table host at the end to share those answers with the whole room.

**Props, Aids, Special Forms**
There needs to be 8 question sheets drawn up (the question and a number of prompts on each one) and envelopes containing all 8 sheets made up for passing to the table hosts. There are numerous business-related questions

which could be asked, and lots of prompts for each question. Here are some suggested examples: -

***Question 1***
***What mistake have you made in the last 2 weeks – and what have you learned from that mistake?***
Have you targeted a marketing activity incorrectly?
Have you made a pricing error?
Have you delivered an unprepared presentation?
Have you chosen the wrong supplier?
Have you engaged the wrong employee?

***Question 2***
***What new business tool or technique have you discovered in the last 4 weeks – and how has this helped you in your business?***
Have you been shown how to do something new in Word, Excel or Powerpoint?
Have you been shown how to make more use of Social Media?
Have you seen a new HR package?
Have you been introduced to a Mastermind, Coaching or Mentoring group?
Have you learned how to make your data safer?

***Question 3***
***What new business contacts have you made in the last 2 weeks – and how might they help your business?***
Potential clients
New suppliers
Potential collaborators
Advisers, coaches, consultants
Experts

***Question 4***

***What business successes have you achieved in the last 2 weeks – and how can you repeat them?***

New clients
Big order from existing client
Cost reduction
Simplification of a process or system
Accreditation, approval, testimonial, endorsement

***Question 5***

***How have you developed as a business person in the last 6 months – and what do you put this development down to?***

More confident presenter
Better negotiator – selling or buying
Better leader, manager, delegator, organiser, motivator
Due to training courses, seminars, books, online articles
Influenced by experts, authors, other business people, colleagues, staff, family

***Question 6***

***Which business person has inspired you in the last 6 months – and how differently have you behaved as a result?***

Famous entrepreneurs, inventors, leaders, authors, gurus
Speakers, Presenters, Facilitators
Other local business people
Effect – implemented new technique or idea, even a new motto or slogan
Effect – acted more decisively, became better organised, started planning

***Question 7***
***What 3 key pieces of advice would you give to someone starting up a new business like yours?***
Marketing – methods, timing, measurement, branding and positioning
Organisations to join, business support
Funding, investing, loans, cash flow
Budgetting, forecasting, managing expectations
Staffing – full-time or part-time, permanent or temporary, skills and training
Legal – contracts, Ts & Cs, intellectual property

***Question 8***
***Which opportunity have you missed in the last 6 months, and how can you ensure you don't miss similar opportunities in the future?***
Failed to bid or tender for a piece of business
Missed advertising or sponsorship slot
Lost an important member of staff
Failed to spot the rise of an innovative new competitor
Missed a chance to diversify
Too late to notice the availability of a new office, warehouse, showroom etc

**Takeaways**
Delegates will have picked up some useful tips from their fellow networkers and should try to incorporate at least 3 things to address in their "To Do" list.

This exercise can work well by just asking one question to everyone in a small group. Question 1 above would serve that purpose, as it is the most likely to generate a wide variety of answers.

## PART 8 (xiii) NETWORKING BINGO

**Overview**
This is perhaps the most low-brow networking format I have organised – but it is enormously popular, competitive and good fun. Just think of embellishing a round of elevator pitches with seaside tackiness, sticks of rock and "Kiss Me Quick" hats! Networkers all get the chance to deliver their elevator pitches but they do not get called up in any particular order – instead a bingo machine determines who gets to speak next. To be successful, it needs a decent number of participants – at least 25 people and at least 5 tables.

**Objectives**
As well as delivering their elevator pitches, delegates can expect to have a bit of fun and maybe win a prize (although their expectations here should be managed!).

**Announcement**
This is a down-market, seaside, "kiss-me-quick" version of networking which includes a game of bingo. It can often be an ordeal for networkers as their turn to speak creeps up on them – they panic, feverishly rehearse their elevator pitch and don't listen to the previous couple of speakers.
At this meeting, the next speaker is determined by the random appearance of a numbered ball from a bingo machine. Whilst numbers are called out, each table fills in a jumbo-sized bingo card – and there is a "tacky" prize for the winning table. After the break, the bingo machine is used again to determine the pairings for some one-to-one sessions.

**Delegate Briefing**

This is a down-market, seaside, "kiss-me-quick" version of networking. Nevertheless, you will all get the chance to stand up and tell everyone else what you do. At many of our meetings we enable pitches to the room, organised on a table-by-table basis. For this event, the identity of the next person to speak will be determined by the appearance of a numbered ball from a bingo machine. Each table will have a large bingo card, upon which to cover those numbers called out – and the first table to cover all their numbers will win a "tacky" prize. So "eyes down" for networking with a difference!

**Table Host Briefing**

There are no table hosts at this event.

**Method**

As a preamble, a 10 minutes presentation on the history of bingo (with useful dates and numbers) goes down well and sets the scene. The main exercise takes longer than a normal round of elevator pitches, so you may need to reduce the allotted time each speaker gets.

Find out which delegates have turned up unexpectedly and allocate numbers to them over and above those numbers on the list of delegates. Alternatively, you could just issue cloakroom tickets in numerical order as delegates arrive. The point is that each person has a unique number – and those numbers will correspond with the numbered balls in the bingo machine.

Try to arrange things so that the number of people per table is uniform. Allocate one bingo card and one marker pen to each table and get one person per table to be the "card marker".

Turn the handle on the bingo machine.

Read out the number on the ball which has popped out. Participants with that number on their bingo cards mark their cards accordingly.
The ball is placed in the tray of "used" balls.
The delegate whose number has been called out then delivers their elevator pitch to the room.
This is repeated until one table's card is completed with markings and the relevant table shouts "Bingo!"
The winning card is checked against the ball tray and if all the numbers have been called, that table is declared the winner. If two tables finish on the same number, the first call of "Bingo!" will be the winner – but prepare yourself for controversy if you only have one set of prizes!
Even after a winner has been declared, the exercise continues until all balls have been called and all delegates have presented.
Participants on the winning table are then presented with their "goodie bags" of prizes

**Props, Aids, Special Forms**
This exercise requires a lot of preparation and quite a few special props.
Firstly, a decent quality bingo machine is needed. It should be sufficiently robust to withstand lots of use and not to wobble about the table when being turned. Avoid using lower-quality versions which are no more than toys.
Each machine will come with a ball tray, on which to place the already called balls, and usually 90 numbered balls. It is unlikely that your meeting will attract anything like 90 attendees, so remove those balls numbered above your likely attendance figure – otherwise you will spend half of your time calling out numbers of people not present.

The bingo machine can be used later at the same meeting to decide pairings for one-to-one sessions.

Each table will need a unique bingo card and the numbers on the cards should correspond to the number of balls in play, to give everyone the same chance of winning. Take time to think through the numbers here – I often used 7 cards each containing 14 numbers. Each card was unique but the numbers 1-49 were used twice. This could result in two tables finishing on the same number, although it is unlikely.
In this instance, even if only 35 take part, you still need to include balls numbered above 35 because the cards still include those higher numbers.

|  | 10 |  |  | 31 | 39 |  |
|---|---|---|---|---|---|---|
| 2 |  | 18 | 22 |  |  | 44 |
|  | 14 |  |  | 35 | 41 | 47 |
| 4 |  | 20 | 27 |  |  |  |

|  | 9 |  |  | 32 | 40 |  |
|---|---|---|---|---|---|---|
| 1 |  | 15 | 24 |  |  | 46 |
|  | 12 |  |  | 33 | 42 | 48 |
| 7 |  | 21 | 28 |  |  |  |

|  | 11 |  |  | 34 | 38 |  |
|---|---|---|---|---|---|---|
| 3 |  | 15 | 26 |  |  | 45 |
|  | 13 |  |  | 35 | 41 | 49 |
| 4 |  | 19 | 28 |  |  |  |

|  | 8 |  |  | 30 | 37 |  |
|---|---|---|---|---|---|---|
| 2 |  | 17 | 24 |  |  | 43 |
|  | 11 |  |  | 34 | 42 | 49 |
| 7 |  | 21 | 27 |  |  |  |

|  | 9 |  |  | 29 | 38 |  |
|---|---|---|---|---|---|---|
| 1 |  | 16 | 22 |  |  | 45 |
|  | 13 |  |  | 32 | 40 | 48 |
| 6 |  | 20 | 25 |  |  |  |

|  | 8 |  |  | 31 | 36 |  |
|---|---|---|---|---|---|---|
| 3 |  | 18 | 23 |  |  | 43 |
|  | 12 |  |  | 33 | 39 | 46 |
| 5 |  | 19 | 26 |  |  |  |

|  | 10 |  |  | 29 | 36 |  |
|---|---|---|---|---|---|---|
| 5 |  | 16 | 23 |  |  | 44 |
|  | 14 |  |  | 30 | 37 | 47 |
| 6 |  | 17 | 25 |  |  |  |

To get into the spirit of things, you will need a set of bingo calls. There are several lists of suggested calls on the Internet, but here is the list I worked with (I never needed more than 65).

## NETWORKING BINGO

| No. | Description | No. | Description | No. | Description |
|---|---|---|---|---|---|
| 1 | Kelly's Eye | 26 | Half A Crown | 51 | Bang On The Drum |
| 2 | One Little Duck | 27 | Stairway To Heaven | 52 | Weeks In The Year |
| 3 | It's A Crowd | 28 | Two Stones | 53 | Here Comes Herbie |
| 4 | Knock At The Door | 29 | Wall Street Crash | 54 | Clean The Floor |
| 5 | Olympic Rings | 30 | Speed Limit | 55 | Snakes Alive |
| 6 | Half A Dozen | 31 | Days In The Month | 56 | Marriage Licence |
| 7 | Potting The Black | 32 | Adult Teeth | 57 | Heinz Varieties |
| 8 | Maids-A-Milking | 33 | All The Threes | 58 | Make 'em Wait |
| 9 | Centre Forward | 34 | Phoning Spain | 59 | Brighton Line |
| 10 | PM's Den | 35 | Duck And Dive | 60 | Diamond Jubilee |
| 11 | Legs | 36 | Three Dozen | 61 | Baker's Bun |
| 12 | Dirty Dozen | 37 | Roulette Slots | 62 | Tickety Boo |
| 13 | Unlucky For Some | 38 | Premier League Games | 63 | Queen Bee |
| 14 | Valentine's Day | 39 | Number Of Steps | 64 | Paul McCartney |
| 15 | Rugby Team | 40 | Double Top | 65 | OAP |
| 16 | Sweet Little Sixteen | 41 | Life's Begun | | |
| 17 | Dancing Queen | 42 | Winnie The Pooh | | |
| 18 | Able To Vote | 43 | Dodgy Knee | | |
| 19 | Goodbye Teens | 44 | All The Fours | | |
| 20 | One Score | 45 | Cowboy's Friend | | |
| 21 | Key Of The Door | 46 | Pick And Mix | | |
| 22 | Bishop Desmond | 47 | Kalashnikov | | |
| 23 | Thee And Me | 48 | Four Dozen | | |
| 24 | Blackbirds | 49 | PC | | |
| 25 | Quarter Century | 50 | Bullseye | | |

You may wish to invest in a seaside hat, complete with "Miss Me Quick" or similar printed slogan, although it may be difficult finding any other suitable occasion to wear it!
And, finally, in the true bingo fashion, you will need to provide prizes for the winning table. You can take the easy way out and just award one item (bar of chocolate, bottle of wine, assortment of biscuits) to each participant on the winning table. But I found it better to award "goodie bags" to the winners. Get a number of the bags you use at children's parties and fill them with cheap, silly items. Items we used were packs of post-its, pens, chocolate bars, mini bottles of wine, finger spinners, memory sticks, crossword books, mouse mats, scribble pads, mini sticks of rock and mini packets of biscuits. Make sure you have enough bags for the highest number you are likely to get on one table.

**Takeaways**

Delegates will have had fun during the evening, they will have had the chance to pitch their business to the room and they will have had the chance to network with the other networkers.

## PART 8 (xiv) NETWORKING SAFARI

**Overview**

This activity works best when the Networking Safari is followed after a break by the Networking Jungle presentation. But they can be run on their own. The Safari enables delegates to pitch their businesses to other delegates and to find out more about the other participants. The Jungle identifies types of networker (likened to animals) and how they should be handled. The exercise is full of good practical networking tips and is always enjoyed by the participants.

**Objectives**

Delegates should attend this activity with the intention of learning a few new networking techniques. They will also find out how good they are at listening.

**Announcement**

This networking format is called "Safari" because it involves a few movements – followed by a nasty sting in the tail.

You will be asked to network with a number of other delegates, according to a route which you are given – avoiding all things nasty of course. But then, just when you think you are in the clear, you will be asked to do something you are not expecting – just like it happens in the jungle, and just like it happens in business.

Continuing with the "Safari" theme, after the break you will be introduced to the Networking Jungle. You will recognise a number of beasts you meet at networking events and you will be taught how to deal with each of them. Come along and learn how to deal with that most deadly networking beast, the Boa Constrictor!

Safari suits and loin cloths are not compulsory.

**Delegate Briefing**

Loin cloths and safari suits are recommended for this event – but they are not compulsory!

The format gets its name because it involves movement followed by stings, some mild and some nasty. When proceeding comfortably on a safari it is likely that you will be confronted by something unexpected – just like being in business. We will re-create that scenario by throwing some surprises your way.

During the first half of the meeting you will meet other delegates at three or four different tables, exchanging 60 second pitches with them all. After everyone has pitched to their table, you will be confronted with something you are not expecting – let's just say it will test how well you have been listening.

After the break, we will venture all the way into the Networking Jungle, meeting various networking beasts whose behaviour you must address if the value of your networking is not to be affected.

Among others, you will meet the Boa Constrictor and the Cheetah!

**Table Host Briefing**

Table hosts are not required for this activity.

**Method**

Firstly, ask all delegates to point at the person on their table who will deliver the first pitch. Get those people to start their pitches and get your stopwatch running. After the allotted time, clap your hands to signify that it is now someone else's turn. And so on, around the table. Not all tables will have the same number of delegates, in which case wait for the final table to finish.

While the final delegates are speaking, place the small printed movement cards on each table. After everyone has had the chance to present, the first “Minor Sting In The Tail” takes place. Going around, table by table, a guest or new member is asked to stand up. A volunteer from that table is then requested to get up and present the standing person’s business to the room. After each table has done that, delegates are ready to move on to their second table. Each delegate takes one card from the pile and is instructed to take themself, their belongings and their small printed card to the table corresponding with the second letter on their movement card. When the movements have all taken place, check that everyone has their movement card with them and that they are sitting at the table corresponding with their second letter. They then go around the table, 60 seconds each, until everyone has had a turn. After they have all finished, the second “Minor Sting In The Tail” takes place. Select other guests or new members (not those already selected) and again call for volunteers to present those delegates’ businesses to the room.

After each table has had its turn, ask all delegates to pass their cards to the people sitting on their immediate left. Everyone now has a different card in their hand and they should be instructed to move to the table corresponding to the first letter on their card. They then go around the table again, 60 seconds each, until everyone has had a turn. After they have all finished, the “Nasty Sting In The Tail” takes place.

Every delegate then gets 60 seconds to present to their table – but this time they are presenting the business two places to the right of them. This keeps delegates on their toes and checks how well they have been listening. Before this round starts, check that no colleagues are two places apart – if they are, move one so they are now sitting next to each other.

After the Safari has ended, and after a break, the delegates can be taken all the way into the Networking Jungle. This is predominantly a slide presentation which recognises "networking beasts" from their behaviour or demeanour – and suggests ways in which other networkers should handle such people. The exercise can consist merely of one slide per beast and maybe a summary, but it works best if it incorporates mini exercises like "The Birthday Line" and "Thanks For The Memory" with explanations on ice-breaking techniques and formulating an elevator pitch.

There is no limit to the number of beasts covered but it can be made more impactful by including pictures of the beasts and sound effects (there are many downloadable free animal sounds on the Internet). I even managed to find a Tarzan cry for effect!

As each slide appears, it should be explained what networking behaviour applies to each beast, and why that is bad (except for the spider, which has good behaviour). The next point is how networkers can help that beast to improve or change their behaviour. For example, the White Rabbit is so called because it is always late. Other networkers must point out that turning up late creates a very poor impression of the business, so punctuality must be addressed.

At the beginning of each Jungle presentation, I played "The Lion Sleeps Tonight" and finished up with "Jungle Rock", both of which contributed to a fun networking event.

**Props, Aids, Special Forms**

If the organiser can acquire a safari hat, it sets the tone for the evening – a full safari suit is a bit over the top!

I used to throw a rubber snake into the group at the start of the presentation to liven things up.

Large A4 printed table cards should be used to clearly indicate the letter of each table, preferably on clear plastic menu holders.

Small printed movement cards should be used to indicate at which tables the delegates will sit.

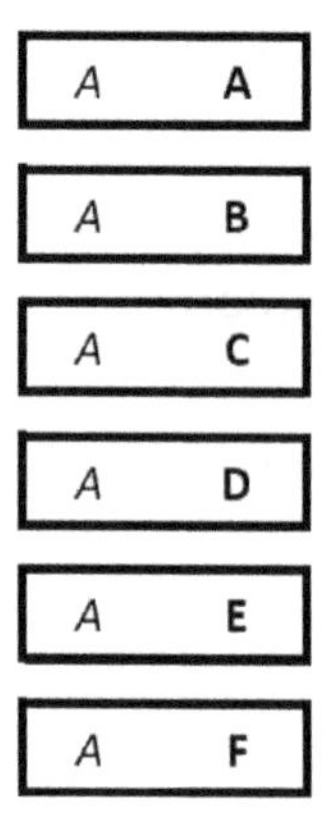


Printing these cards in colour, say red on the left and blue on the right, helps to explain the process.

And a set of presentation slides, one per "beast" should be prepared. Each slide should contain a picture of the "beast", the name of the "beast" and 3 distinctive characteristics – which of course apply to the networking beast as well as to the creature in the jungle.

***White Rabbit***
Disorganised
Always late to arrive
"Sorry I'm Late"
***Flamingo***
Arrive with their friends
Stay with their friends
Leave with their friends
***Porcupine***
Stand on their own
Clam up when approached
Slow to open up
***Boa Constrictor***
Really dangerous
Refuse to let go
Squeeze the life out of you
***Lion***
Always the predator
Hunt down the other attendees
Can be overpowering
***Kookaburra***
Over talkative
Difficult to shut up
Distracting
***Leopard***
Can't change their spots
Not open to new ideas
Reluctant to change
***Cheetah***
Fastest of all beasts
Very quick off the mark

Difficult to tie down
***Spider***
Very patient
Very persistent
Never gives up

Other possibilities:-
***Swan*** – very monogamistic, sticking to just one networking group
***Monkey*** – very fun-loving, but don't take things seriously enough
***Chick*** – brand new on the networking scene, needing help and guidance
***Owl*** – seasoned and very wise networker
***Magpie*** – collects business cards and freebies, without following up
***Mayfly*** – float in and out of events without "getting how networking works"

**Takeaways**
The Safari will have taught the delegates about their listening skills. The Jungle will have taught the delegates a few new techniques which will help to make their networking more effective.

## PART 8 (xv) OPEN AND CLOSED

**Overview**
Effective business networkers spend more time asking questions than pitching their own businesses. But the questioning process can be far more fruitful if you know the difference between open and closed questioning – and how to use them both. This exercise teaches delegates the difference between the two types of questioning and enables them to use both techniques in a couple of practical exercises.

**Objectives**
Delegates should be prepared to learn about different questioning techniques and then satisfy themselves that they can put these into practice.

**Announcement**
Our next meeting features an exercise looking at the effectiveness of open and closed questioning.
As networkers, we recognise the need to gather information about each other's businesses – but how should we go about requesting that information? We will run a fun exercise to illustrate the difference between open and closed questions – and then you will apply those lessons to an actual business situation.

**Delegate Briefing**
This is an exercise all about questioning techniques and is designed to illustrate the effectiveness of open and closed questions. After a presentation on the two different techniques, all delegates will be put into pairs for the rest of the exercise.

To begin with, delegates will use the two types of questions to arrive at the identity of mystery people. One of you will only ask closed questions and the other will only ask open questions. You will then apply the lessons learned to a business setting – using both types of questions to really drill down and understand more about each other's businesses.
Apart from knowing far more about each other's businesses, you will take away a clear understanding of the effectiveness of open and closed questions.

**Table Host Briefing**
It is not necessary to appoint table hosts for this activity.

**Method**
To set the scene, run a brief presentation on the difference between Open and Closed Questioning.
Arrange delegates into pre-determined pairs (try to make up the pairs on their existing tables, avoiding any previous 121 pairings).
Each delegate takes a sticky label and writes the name of a famous person (living or dead) on the label. The idea is that each delegate sticks their label on their partner's forehead and the partner has to guess whose name is on their forehead.
Person 1 has a sticker on their forehead, they ask closed questions to identify the name of the famous person on their sticker.
Person 2 has a sticker on their forehead, they ask open questions to identify the name of the famous person on their sticker (not to use obvious questions like "Who Am I?" or "What Does It Say On My Sticky Label?")

Person 1 then has 5 minutes to ask closed questions about Person 2's business – and then 5 minutes to ask open questions.
Person 2 then has 5 minutes to ask closed questions about Person 1's business – and then 5 minutes to ask open questions.

**Props, Aids, Special Forms**
Run a few slides on the difference between the two types of questioning, stressing that closed questions only invite 3 answers – Yes, No and Don't Know. Try to include the following useful questions: -

7 Killer Open Questions To Understand Someone's Business

- What does your business do
- When did you start doing this?
- Where are you based?
- Why are your products or services different?
- Who are your customers?
- Which methods do you use to find new customers?
- How can I help you?

7 Useful and Time-Saving Closed Questions

- Do you employ anyone?
- Do you have a website?
- Are you based locally?
- Can I connect with you on LinkedIn?
- Will you be attending the next XYZ meeting?
- Is it ok to send you some details by e-mail?

Provide sticky labels for delegates to write on, preferably already cut up but with their backings still on. Maybe the

"7 Killer Questions" slide could be left on the screen while the questioning exercise proceeds.

**Takeaways**

Delegates will have picked up a very useful business tool which will enhance their networking experience.

## PART 8 (xvi) PAIR AND SHARE

**Overview**
This is a structured event which amplifies the importance of selling "through" the room by succinctly and memorably passing on messages so that other people can convey details of a networker's business to others.
It is also a test of networkers' listening skills.

**Objectives**
Delegates should attend this session with the intention of (a) developing new networking techniques and (b) learning more about other networkers' businesses.

**Announcement**
Effective networking is of fundamental importance to us and we often discuss the importance of selling through the room and not selling to the room. Therefore, we have to be sure that our sales message is understood by our fellow networkers, so that they can effectively convey that message to the people they meet outside of the room.
At this highly-participative meeting we are going to test: -

- how good are you at understanding someone else's business?
- how effectively can you present someone else's business?
- how easy is your pitch to understand?

After the break we will organise two one-to-one sessions which will enable you to really drill down and identify how fellow networkers can help each other.

**Delegate Briefing**

This meeting is very different from our other formats. It should be fun, but there is nevertheless a strong business reason for doing it. Effective networking is of fundamental importance and we have often discussed the importance of selling through the room and not selling to the room. Therefore we have to be sure that our sales message is understood by our fellow networkers, so that they can effectively convey that message to people they meet outside of the room.

At this meeting, we are going to test: -

- how good are you at understanding someone else's business?
- how effectively can you present someone else's business to the room?
- how easy is it for another networker to understand your sales message?

You will be placed in pairs and you will be given 10 minutes (5 minutes each) to ask questions of each other and ensure you understand each other's business. Each person will then present the other person's business to the rest of the room.

If your business message cannot easily be passed on outside of the networking room, then your networking will simply not be effective. Therefore, afterwards, you should consider how your sales pitch can be improved, so that other networkers can better convey it to third parties.

After the break we will organise two one-to-one sessions which will enable you to really drill down and identify how fellow networkers can help each other.

**Table Host Briefing**

No table hosts are necessary for this event.

**Method**

As delegates arrive, allocate them to four groups – Red, Blue, Yellow and Green. The exercise works best when there is an even number of delegates, but a group of three can be used for either part of the meeting.

The first part of the evening is used for delegates to present their own businesses just to the other members of their colour group (ideally 60 seconds each).

The second part is the "Pair" exercise. Create pairs of people by getting the "Red" people to match up with "Blue" people and the "Yellow" people to match up with the "Green" people. Each pair spends 10 minutes together, learning about each other's business. They then return to their original seats.

One by one each delegate stands up and the person they paired with presents the other person's business to the room. This continues until all delegates have presented. This can often be very amusing as some delegates pretend to be each other!

At the end of the "Pair" exercise, delegates are asked to consider how they might want to change their pitches in future so that other people will find it easier to pass on their details. In other words, how can they be more "memorable"?

After the break, the third part of the meeting is the first "Share" session. Get the "Red" people to match up with the "Yellow" people and the "Blue" people to match up with the "Green" people. Each pair then has 15 minutes to learn more about the other person's business – but without having to present to the room this time.

The final part is the second "Share" session. Get the "Red" people to match up with the "Green" people and the "Blue" people to match up with the "Yellow" people. Each pair then has 15 minutes to learn more about the other person's business – again without having to present to the room.

For the "Share" one-to-one sessions, give delegates a simple agenda. After each session they should ask: -

- Do I understand their business?
- Do I understand what they are seeking?
- How am I going to help them?

**Props, Aids, Special Forms**

On the groups' tables, use 4 menu card holders containing cards in the four colours.

You may also choose to issue coloured lapel stickers as delegates check in. This makes it easier to find a partner with whom to pair.

**Takeaways**

Networkers will go away knowing more about how easy they are to be passed on, and they may well modify their future pitches accordingly. They will also have got to know a lot more about some other networkers' businesses.

## PART 8 (xvii) SEND THREE AND FOURPENCE

**Overview**

This exercise requires a lot of preparation and needs to be run with almost military precision!
It is a kind of networking "Chinese Whispers" activity, designed to illustrate the importance of developing a succinct and memorable pitch. There is a lot of movement and a lot of fun – but it does make a serious point about being easy to pass on.

**Objectives**

Delegates should enter this process with the aim of finding out how effective their pitch is.

**Announcement**

Forget the idea of a relaxing session - this is just about the hardest work you will ever get through at a networking event! After much card-passing, colour-coding and movement, the fourth person in the chain gets to present your business to the room. There will be lots of physical movement and plenty of fun, but there is a serious point underneath it all – how well does your business message travel through a network of contacts?
Two other networking sessions sandwich the main event, making this the most active networking event you'll attend – and we will start with a piece on Trench Warfare, just to set the scene. We promise you'll enjoy it.

**Delegate Briefing**

Fundamental to your success as a networker is the effectiveness of your presentation, or "elevator pitch". Once finished, you should be confident that your message has been understood and that everyone in the room is able to go forth and pass on details of your business to the people they meet. We are going to test just how effective you are by passing on your message and then by asking someone else down the line to present your business to the room.

When you arrive you will be designated as a "Red", "Blue", "Yellow" or "Green" person. Your name and business appear on a card of that colour – as does your lapel badge.

During this exercise you will be moved around the room, depending upon your designated colour, and you will be asked to "pair up" with someone else of certain designated colours.

Listen to instructions, only move when asked to do so and only commence speaking when you receive the signal to do so.

You will present your own business for 60 seconds to one other person and you will subsequently present 2 other businesses to other people. You will also receive 3 presentations yourself from other individuals.

After this exercise, you will resume your seats and you will be holding the card of someone 3 steps removed from you in the chain. It is this business which you will present to the room when called upon.

You will have 60 seconds to present the business represented by the card in your possession – and somewhere in the room your business will be presented by whoever is holding your card.

By the time your business is presented to the room, it will have been initially presented by you and then it will have passed to 2 further contacts – as our pitches are passed on in real life.

Remember "It Is Not Who You Know That Counts – It Is Who Knows You" – so, listen closely to the way your business is presented and ask yourself: -

- Was my business represented accurately?
- Was my message clearly understood?
- Were my USPs stressed?
- Was something important omitted?

After every business has been presented, you will be asked to consider how you might change your pitch in future, so it can be passed on more effectively.

**Table Host Briefing**
There are no table hosts at this event.

**Method**
Before the meeting, take cards of 4 colours (red, blue, yellow and green) and cut them up into smaller cards (about 90mm x 60mm). Make sure you have as many small cards as the expected number of delegates – plus a few spares of course. Put the small cards in a pile and put them in order – red, blue, yellow, green, red, blue etc. Either print (this is better, if you can) or handwrite the names and businesses of all the delegates onto sheets of white adhesive labels. Use labels which are small enough to fit on the small cards you have prepared. Acquire packs of small (22mm x 16mm) lapel labels and lay them out ready for the registration process.
When each delegate arrives, find their name and business on the sheet of adhesive labels, then peel off their label and attach it to the next coloured card on the pile (the first delegate will get a red card, the second delegate will get a blue card, and so on. Also, attach one of the small lapel

labels to the delegate's lapel (or similar) – this lapel sticker will be the same colour as the card they have just received.
Each table (or group of tables) should have an upright clear plastic menu card holder bearing cards of the four colours. Delegates sit initially at the table bearing the colour of their cards and lapel stickers.
The first exercise invites the delegates to get to know people who are in the same colour group as themselves. Around the group, 60 seconds each, until everyone has had their turn.
At that stage, run the slideshow which will explain from where the event gets its name. Then the fun starts!
There are six rounds whereby delegates are presenting their own and other people's businesses to each other. It is really important that delegates listen to instructions, only moving and speaking when instructed to do so. Here is the running order of instructions: -

Round 1
Check that everyone has hold of their coloured card (with their name and business on it).
Red people pair up with Blue people and Yellow people pair up with Green people.
For 60 seconds, Reds present their own businesses to the Blues and Yellows present their own businesses to the Greens. At the same time, Reds present their Red cards to the Blues and Yellows present their Yellow cards to the Greens.
Before moving on, check that Reds now have no cards, Blues have Red and Blue cards, Yellows have no cards and Greens have Yellow and Green cards.

Round 2

Red people pair up with Green people and Yellow people pair up with Blue people.
For 60 seconds, Greens present the businesses on the Yellow cards they are holding to the Reds and Blues present the businesses on the Red cards they are holding to the Yellows. At the same time, Greens and Blues pass over the cards of the businesses being presented.
Before moving on, check that Reds now have Yellow cards, Blues have Blue cards, Yellows have Red cards and Greens have Green cards.

Round 3
Red people pair up with Blue people and Yellow people pair up with Green people.
For 60 seconds, Reds present the businesses on the Yellow cards they are holding to the Blues and Yellows present the businesses on the Red cards they are holding to the Greens. At the same time, Reds and Yellows pass over the cards of the businesses being presented.
Before moving on, check that Reds now have no cards, Blues have Blue and Yellow cards, Yellows have no cards and Greens have Green and Red cards.

Round 4
Red people pair up with Green people and Yellow people pair up with Blue people.
For 60 seconds, Greens present their own businesses to the Reds and Blues present their own businesses to the Yellows. At the same time, Greens present their Green cards to the Reds and Blues present their Blue cards to the Yellows.
Before moving on, check that Reds now have Green cards, Blues have Yellow cards, Yellows have Blue cards and Greens have Red cards.

Round 5
Red people pair up with Blue people and Yellow people pair up with Green people.
For 60 seconds, Yellows present the businesses on the Blue cards they are holding to the Greens and Reds present the businesses on the Green cards they are holding to the Blues. At the same time, Yellows and Reds pass over the cards of the businesses being presented.
Before moving on, check that Reds now have no cards, Blues have Yellow and Green cards, Yellows have no cards and Greens have Red and Blue cards.

Round 6
Red people pair up with Green people and Yellow people pair up with Blue people.
For 60 seconds, Greens present the businesses on the Blue cards they are holding to the Reds and Blues present the businesses on the Green cards they are holding to the Yellows. At the same time, Greens and Blues pass over the cards of the businesses being presented.
For the final time, check that Reds now have Blue cards, Blues have Yellow cards, Yellows have Green cards and Greens have Red cards. All delegates then return to their original seats.

Round 7
Choose any delegate in the Red group and ask them to stand up. Then ask for that person's business to be presented by whoever in the room is now holding that Red card (it will be a Green person).
After that Green person has finished the presentation, ask them to stay standing. And then ask for that Green

business to be presented by whoever in the room is holding the relevant card (it will be a Yellow person). Carry on until everyone has presented. If you end up with the first Red person again, then just choose a different Red person to re-start the chain.

Round 8

To conclude the event, delegates can be invited to share their takeaways with the rest of their group. They can discuss how they might change their pitches in future, in order to be easier to remember.

Alternatively, delegates can pair up with those groups they have not yet met – so Reds meet Yellows and Blues meet Greens – for a 15 minutes one-to-one session.

**Props, Aids, Special Forms**

You need 4 coloured cards (A4) to stand up in clear plastic holders to signify where the respective groups sit at the start and again after the movements have finished.

You need similar coloured cards, cut up into small 90 x 60mm cards.

You also need small 22 x 16mm lapel stickers for delegates to wear.

Prepare a brief slide presentation showing where the event title comes from. Include images of trench warfare, the need for "trench runners" who took messages between the front line and the senior officers and refer to Adolf Hitler's relative success as a "trench runner". Explain how "Send reinforcements, going to advance" was allegedly delivered as "Send three and fourpence, going to a dance".

A control sheet, itemising the various rounds and the cards held by each group, should be used as should a guide to what happens if the total delegates is not a multiple of 4.

| Round | Details of Activity | | | | |
|---|---|---|---|---|---|
| 1 | R | presents | R | to | B |
| 1 | Y | presents | Y | to | G |
| 2 | B | presents | R | to | Y |
| 2 | G | presents | Y | to | R |
| 3 | Y | presents | R | to | G |
| 3 | R | presents | Y | to | B |
| 4 | B | presents | B | to | Y |
| 4 | G | presents | G | to | R |
| 5 | Y | presents | B | to | G |
| 5 | R | presents | G | to | B |
| 6 | G | presents | B | to | R |
| 6 | B | presents | G | to | Y |

| Cards Held At End Of Each Round | | | | |
|---|---|---|---|---|
| | **R** | **B** | **Y** | **G** |
| **1** | Nil | R & B | Nil | Y & G |
| **2** | Y | B | R | G |
| **3** | Nil | B & Y | Nil | G & R |
| **4** | G | Y | B | R |
| **5** | Nil | Y & G | Nil | R & B |
| **6** | B | Y | G | R |

***SEND THREE AND FOURPENCE – if there is no multiple of 4***

ONE OVER
No participation in rounds 1-6
Presents own business to the room at the very end of the exercise
Or ask two colleagues to participate as one

TWO OVER
No participation in rounds 1-4
Round 5 – A presents own business to B
Round 6 – B presents own business to A
A then presents B to the room and B presents A to the room at the very end of the exercise

THREE OVER
Round 1 A presents own business to B (using own business cards) – C sits out
Round 2 B presents A's business to C – A sits out
Round 3 C presents own business to A (using own business cards) – B sits out
Round 4 A presents C's business to B – C sits out
Round 5 B presents own business to C (using own business cards) – A sits out
Round 6 C presents B's business to A – B sits out
A presents B's business, B presents C's business, C presents A's business to the room at the end

**Takeaways**
Delegates will have had fun at this lively event but they should also go away with thoughts of how they could enhance their elevator pitches in order to be memorable.

# PART 8 (xviii) SPANISH INQUISITION

**Overview**

Networkers normally stand up and tell other networkers about their businesses. But they say what they think the other people ought to hear – and not necessarily what the listeners want to know. So this exercise gives delegates the chance to ask what they want to know about each other's businesses. And then we check how well people listen to other delegates' pitches.

**Objectives**

Delegates can learn what other people want to know about them and may alter their pitches accordingly. They can also look forward to learning more about the other delegates.

**Announcement**

Our next meeting is an exercise in Interrogation and Torture!

Business networking is not blatant selling – it is all about building relationships and collaborating. A fundamental skill in networking is that of asking effective and probing questions.

The first half of the meeting tests our questioning skills. Everyone gets chance to have their business revealed to their table – but the information given out is not that which we want to present, it is that which the other participants have asked for.

In the second half we test our listening skills, but with a cruel twist – which is where an element of torture comes in!

**Delegate Briefing**

Fundamental to your success as a networker is the effectiveness of your questioning. Networking is not a blatant sales pitch, it is the development of mutually-beneficial business relationships. In order to help other businesses, it is important to fully understand exactly what features and benefits they offer. Only by good questioning can you get a full understanding. In this exercise we are going to test just how effective your questioning is by getting you to drill down until you get a clear understanding of what other members offer. This will enable us to help each other more effectively.

You will be placed on a table with 5 or 6 other businesses, arranged so that there is a good mix of business sectors and levels of experience. Each business will have 10 minutes to (a) give a brief "elevator pitch" to the rest of the table and (b) to be questioned by the other businesses who seek to know more.

Whilst each business is making its initial pitch, the other people on the table should make notes, along the lines of: -

- do I understand exactly what the product is?
- are the customer benefits identified?
- who are the potential or target customers?
- what leads or contacts does this business seek?
- what kind of businesses would make logical alliance partners?
- does this business have competitors?
- what expertise can I offer to this business?
- how can my network of contacts help this business?

The table host will ask the first question, and then each person in turn around the table gets to ask one question. Answers to questions should be clear but brief, to allow

more questions to be asked. Once everyone around the table has had the chance to ask a question, further questions can be asked, at the table host's discretion. Towards the end of the 10 minutes slot, the table host will check that every person on the table has a clear understanding of what the business does. One-to-one follow up meetings can be arranged for interested parties. The next business then takes its turn to be grilled under the spotlight.
At the end of this exercise, you will have gained a clearer understanding of 5 or 6 other businesses and they will have a far better idea of yours. You may also have sown some seeds towards business alliances and collaborations.

After this exercise we will test your listening skills, with a cruel twist thrown in, just to introduce a little torture – which is where the real Spanish Inquisition came in …

**Table Host Briefing**
Fundamental to the success of networkers is the effectiveness of their questioning. In order to help other businesses, it is important to fully understand exactly what features and benefits they offer. Only by good questioning can you get a full understanding. This is an exercise to test just how effective the delegates' questioning is by getting them to drill down until they get a clear understanding of what other members offer.
You will have 5 or 6 other businesses on your table, arranged so that there is a good mix of business sectors and levels of experience. Each business will give a very brief "elevator pitch" to the rest of the table. They must then stop pitching and only answer questions as they have the rest of their 10 minutes to be questioned by the other delegates.

Whilst each business is making its initial pitch, the other people on the table should be considering questions about

- what the product or services does
- customer benefits
- target customers
- what leads or contacts are sought
- logical alliance partners
- competitors
- what sort of help is needed, and how the others can use their contacts

After the initial pitch, you should ask the first question, and then each person in turn around the table gets to ask one question. You must ensure that answers to questions are clear and brief, to allow more questions to be asked. Once everyone around the table has had the chance to ask a question, further questions can be asked, at your discretion. Towards the end of the 10 minutes slot, you should check that every person on the table has a clear understanding of what the business does. One-to-one follow up meetings can be arranged for interested parties. The next business then takes its turn to be grilled under the spotlight.

At the end of this exercise, encourage all the businesses on your table to arrange one-to-one meetings with each other so that they can explore ways of helping each other. In that way we can sow some seeds towards business alliances and collaborations. We then introduce a little torture to the proceedings, whilst checking how good delegates' listening skills are …

**Method**
This activity works best if a seating plan is used – if so, try to keep competing businesses apart, try to obtain a good gender balance and try to spread out the guests and new members. Table hosts are important, so try to use proven facilitators if possible.
There are no elevator pitches to the room, instead businesses are "interrogated" by the other people on their table. Each participant is questioned for ten minutes, the table hosts keeping time and ensuring that everyone gets a fair chance to take part.
Towards the end of the session, each delegate is given a card containing the letter of the table to which they will move for the second part of the exercise, after the break. No two people will then be on the same tables for the second part.
The second exercise is the "torture" part of the evening. Make sure that, if there are any colleagues sitting on the same tables, they are sitting next to each other. Delegates should be warned that they must listen closely to all the presenters for this activity.
Each delegate has 60 seconds to present their own business to the table. Then a further round of presentations takes place – but this time (here comes the torture!) each person must present the business which is two seats to their right!

**Props, Aids, Special Forms**
You will need stand-up table letters printed on cards and displayed in clear plastic menu card holders.
Print a sheet of table letters – enough in total for the expected number of delegates and using letters which correspond with the expected number of tables. Anticipate 5 tables of 5, 6 x 6, 7 x 7 etc.

Present a modest number of slides on the history of The Spanish Inquisition, with images if possible
Try especially to include part of Monty Python's "Spanish Inquisition" sketch from YouTube. Alternatively, just introduce delegates to the Spanish Inquisition using these notes: -

*The Tribunal of the Holy Office of the Inquisition was established in 1478 by Ferdinand II of Aragon and Isabella I of Castile. It was intended to maintain Catholic orthodoxy, and to ensure the orthodoxy of those who converted from Judaism and Islam.*
*The process consisted of a series of hearings, in which both the denouncers and the defendant gave testimony. In order to interrogate the accused, the Inquisition made use of torture, almost developing it into an art form.*
*King Philip II of Spain, inherited the Low Countries from the Duchy of Burgundy. The Dutch Revolt (1568–1648) was the successful revolt of the largely Protestant provinces against the rule of the Roman Catholic Spanish. (The southern Catholic provinces initially joined in the revolt, but later submitted to Spain.)*
*King Philip II implemented a new and very nasty "Spanish Inquisition" in the Netherlands to eliminate Protestantism. Popular literature, pamphlets and other images from the time painted a picture of a widespread, awful "Spanish Inquisition."*
*The religious 'clash of cultures' built up into outbursts of violence. These tensions led to the formation of the independent Dutch state. But the years of the Spanish Inquisition were not the most loved in Dutch history.*
*The comedy show Monty Python's Flying Circus produced a sketch in the early 70s in which people being questioned would calmly state "I didn't expect The Spanish*

*Inquisition". This was greeted with 3 caped cardinals bursting in, exclaiming "Nobody Expects The Spanish Inquisition"*

**Takeaways**

Delegates should get valuable feedback on what other networkers would like to know about their businesses, and they may amend their usual pitches because of that. They will also know how good they are at listening.

## PART 8 (xix) SPEAKER EVENT

**Overview**

A number of networking events are introduced and almost apologetically add the fact that there will be a speaker at the event. "We will do X, Y and Z – and there will be a speaker afterwards". I have always believed that the choice of speaker, and the content, should be used to drive attendees to the event and I would like to share those thoughts here.

**Objectives**

Attendees at events which include speakers should expect to be educated, inspired, entertained – and perhaps all three. They should come with open minds and prepare to receive information which will make them better networkers, better business people, or both.

**Announcement**

It is important to give each speaker event a catchy title, something which catches people's attention and it can be as corny as you like – but not offensive or suggestive. It could be a play on words around the content or the takeaway of the presentation or just a teaser around what the subject might be. This is a chance to be creative and avoid dry old subjects which could put people off.

**Delegate Briefing**

There is usually no need for a delegate briefing, although it is sometimes useful to ask delegates in advance to bring certain thoughts or information with them.

**Table Host Briefing**

There is no need for table hosts at these meetings

**Method**

Frequency – the balance between speaker events and themed or participative events must be decided by the members of a group. I always used to operate clubs on the basis of every other – so speaker event, followed by a participative exercise, followed by a speaker event, and so on. I regularly checked with my members that they were happy with that 50/50 arrangement, which they were. But the ratio in any group must be determined by the punters themselves. It also makes sense not to repeat the actual subjects too frequently.

Speakers – I always tried to engage speakers that I had actually seen myself, indeed one of the reasons I used to attend other events was to check out the speakers for myself. Occasionally I booked speakers who were strongly recommended by trusted members or organisers of other groups – and I got one or two wrong over the years. Those speakers who merely deliver an extended version of their elevator pitch should be avoided, as should those who merely read out their slides. Ideally speakers should be engaged if they can be relied upon to give the delegates two or three new things to do the following day. Business networkers do not want to listen to uninspiring lectures on heavy topics, instead they want to be inspired to do something which will enhance their businesses.
There are many excellent speakers on the business networking circuit who will come along and deliver an excellent presentation without charging a fee. In this case I believe it is only courteous to offer a contribution towards their travelling expenses, and a blind eye should be turned if they finish up their free talk with a couple of slides

which are blatant sales messages. Helping such speakers to sell their books is only right.
Other speakers charge for their services and their engagement depends on the size of your budget. To justify paying a large fee to a speaker, you need to be pretty sure there will be plenty of fee-paying attendees in the room.
Whenever a speaker has delivered a good presentation, they should be praised on social media and recommendations passed on to other groups' organisers.
Most speakers will share their slides with networking groups, but those who don't want to compromise their intellectual property should be respected.

Multiple Speakers – what can work really well is a format whereby you use 3 or 4 members to deliver mini presentations of about 15 minutes each, instead of engaging one sole speaker. This can consist of different topics or there can be a theme – for instance a group of people in the financial sector (pensions, mortgages, insurance, investments) or maybe a group in the "greater IT" sector (cyber security, social media, websites, mobile phones). If you engage a group from the same sector, encourage them to meet beforehand to avoid any duplication.
I once engaged two speakers under the theme "Staying Safe". This involved one speaker talking about online safety, use of passwords, combatting hackers and not sharing PIN data. The other speaker gave a personal self-defence demonstration.

Subject Matter – it is important that attendees are given a good variety of speaker subjects, mixing pure business topics with softer skills. Some presentations should be educational ("how to" sessions) and some should be more thought-provoking (ideas to take away and develop). A typical list of subjects could include: -

- Accountant's view of the Chancellor's budget effects on SMEs
- Local business leader's story and the lessons learned
- Update on social media developments
- Time management
- Cyber security hints and tips
- How to apply NLP and DISC profiling
- Closing a sale
- Data Protection Dos and Don'ts
- Presentational skills
- Guide to local grants and funding
- Cost-effective PR
- Duties and responsibilities of Company Directors

Occasionally a practical presentation (like first aid or self defence) can provide a refreshing change from the usual slide-driven talks.

Preparation – it should be established at the time of booking the speaker where and when the event will take place, when the speaker will start speaking and how long they have for their spot. Understand if the speaker will use slides, flipcharts, videos or sounds – and then make sure that you or the venue has the wherewithal to support these. Find out before the event if the speaker wants to use any other items of stationery, any special seating arrangement or any volunteers. It is important not to leave anything to chance, helping the speaker and yourself to deliver a slick and professional presentation. Calling the speaker a few days before an event will avoid any nasty surprises on the day itself.

Organisation – if the speaker is going to use any presentational slides, videos or YouTube clips, get the speaker to send the items to you a few days before the event. This gives you time to incorporate their items within your overall slide deck, check for errors or glitches and, in some cases, check for suitability of content (avoiding bad language or suggestive items). If the speaker intends to hand out any forms or questionnaires, establish in advance who is going to print them and at what stage they will be issued to the attendees.

Arrange the room so that attendees can see the speaker, hear the speaker and see the presentation. If sound is going to be used, check the position and strength of the speakers beforehand. Check that the lighting in the room allows the presentation to be clearly seen and position any flipcharts so that they do not prevent attendees from seeing the slides. It is essential that all these things are checked well before the event starts, to ensure that the speaker's session goes off smoothly, without any hitches and with the maximum effect.

Confirm all timings with the speaker in advance, check if a Q & A session can be accommodated at the end, check what handouts or links will be available after the talk and discuss how any books etc will be sold at the end. Try to give the speaker an idea of the number of expected attendees, the business sectors in which they operate and the sizes of their businesses. The speaker can then tailor the presentation accordingly.

The speaker should be briefed as to what happens during the rest of the meeting and should be encouraged to be present during any networking activity. Mention should also be made in advance of your stance on the use of bad language.

**Props, Aids, Special Forms**

The props needed are those which are used to facilitate the speaker's presentation – laptop, screen, projector, speakers, flipchart and pens, extension leads etc.
There will also be items specific to the speaker – pull-up display banner, books, questionnaires, handouts etc.

**Takeaways**

If the speaker is properly briefed, the attendees should leave the meeting inspired and fully-prepared to do something differently in their businesses. If they have been entertained and educated then so much the better, but the main point is that they go away with the intention of doing something in a new or different way.

# PART 8 (xx) SPEED NETWORKING

**Overview**

Speed Networking has been around for many years, it is a bit like a business version of Speed Dating – but without the same follow-up! Personally, I have never liked it because it is noisy (at any one point 50% of the attendees are talking), and it is quite gruelling (attendees struggle if they have not taken a bottle of water with them on their route). However, it is very popular with participants and can be set up without too much difficulty. It can make a refreshing change from just going around the room inviting elevator pitches and it is more comfortable for delegates who are nervous of speaking to the whole room. The problem with Speed Networking is that everyone thinks they can just wing it and proceed without too much preparation. For Speed Networking to work well, it needs to be planned and organised. Without planning, delegates can find themselves meeting the same people twice, or maybe just meeting half of the people in the room.

**Objectives**

Delegates will get the chance to tell lots of people about their business and they should pick up a number of new contacts with whom to network.

**Announcement**

This Speed Networking event will enable delegates to present themselves and their businesses to a number of networkers, whilst learning more about the other people. The room will be arranged so that everyone faces another networker and, upon a signal, each pair will exchange pitches (60 seconds each). At the end of each 2 minutes session, the delegates move by one place and then exchange pitches with the new person they are facing. The movements and pitches continue until the end of the event. By this stage, each networker will have met a large number of people and will have a pocketful of business cards with which to follow up. Participants will need plenty of business cards, plenty of stamina and a bottle of water!

**Delegate Briefing**

As a change from our regular networking format, this event involves lots of one-to-one pitches, so no presentations to the whole room this time. This Speed Networking event will enable delegates to present themselves and their businesses to a number of networkers, whilst learning more about the other people. The room will be arranged so that everyone faces another networker and, upon a signal, each pair will exchange pitches (60 seconds each). You should concentrate on making a "memorable" pitch, making it clear what the benefits are of your product or service, and making it clear what help you are seeking. Do not try to cram as much as you can into your 60 seconds, make things easy for other networkers to understand.

At the end of each 2 minutes session, the delegates move by one place and then exchange pitches with the new person they are facing. The movements and pitches continue until the end of the event.

By this stage, each networker will have met a large number of people and will have a pocketful of business cards with which to follow up. You will need plenty of business cards, plenty of stamina and a bottle of water!

**Table Host Briefing**

No table hosts are necessary for this type of meeting.

**Method**
First of all, establish how long the Speed Networking session will last. I have always found that 60 minutes is long enough and any longer ones that I have witnessed have always seen people dropping out after a while. A very decent session can be had from 30 or 45 minutes. Also, establish how long each pitch should take – 60 seconds is ideal, as anything shorter sees the networkers having to move too often. If each delegate has 60 seconds to speak, each pairing takes 2 minutes – so divide the total minutes available by 2, and that is the number of moves in the session.

Then establish which format will be used, and we will look at the various options below.
Whichever format is used, it is important to tell the participants before the start what the ground rules are: -

- Delegates should grab a water for themselves at the start, as this event can be dehydrating
- Upon the signal to start, the first person in each pair presents themselves and their business to the other
- They should hand over their business cards while they are speaking
- At the signal to change over, the first person stops speaking and the second person then has their turn to present themselves and their business – again, handing over business cards while speaking
- At the signal to stop, the second person stops talking and the delegates move one place
- Delegates take all their belongings with them – papers, cards, drinks, food etc.

- Delegates must move swiftly to their new positions to avoid holding everyone else up
- As soon as all delegates are in position, the signal to start is given and the process is repeated

At the end of the session, delegates should be reminded to follow up with all the people they have just met, building relationships with a view to helping each other.

I have seen people use several variations of the following, depending upon the number of delegates and the time available, but I believe these four Speed Networking formats work best. The illustrations assume 20 or 21 participants: -

***Even Number of Participants, Only One Side Moves***
Person 1 starts with Person 20, 2 with 19 etc. After the first pairing, lower side delegates move one place to the left and Person 20 takes up Person 11's position.

| EVEN NUMBER OF PARTICIPANTS - Half the room moves | | | | | | | | | |
|---|---|---|---|---|---|---|---|---|---|
| 1 | 2 | 3 | 4 | 5 | 6 | 7 | 8 | 9 | 10 |
| | | | | | | | | | |
| 20 | 19 | 18 | 17 | 16 | 15 | 14 | 13 | 12 | 11 |

***Odd Number of Participants, Only One Side Moves***
Person 1 starts with Person 21, 2 with 20 etc, and Person 11 sits out the first pairing. After the first pairing, lower side delegates move one place to the left and Person 21 takes up Person 11's position.

| ODD NUMBER OF PARTICIPANTS - Half the room moves, one person is always "out" | | | | | | | | | | |
|---|---|---|---|---|---|---|---|---|---|---|
| 1 | 2 | 3 | 4 | 5 | 6 | 7 | 8 | 9 | 10 | |
| | | | | | | | | | | **11** |
| 21 | 20 | 19 | 18 | 17 | 16 | 15 | 14 | 13 | 12 | |

***Even Number of Participants, Both Sides Move***
Person 1 starts with Person 20, 2 with 19 etc and person 11 is static. After the first pairing, everyone moves one place to their left, except for Person 11 who never moves. Person 10 takes up Person 12's position.

| EVEN NUMBER OF PARTICIPANTS - Everyone moves except for one "static" person | | | | | | | | | |
|---|---|---|---|---|---|---|---|---|---|
| 1 | 2 | 3 | 4 | 5 | 6 | 7 | 8 | 9 | 10 |
| | | | | | | | | | |
| 20 | 19 | 18 | 17 | 16 | 15 | 14 | 13 | 12 | **11** |

***Odd Number of Participants, Both Sides Move***
Person 1 starts with Person 21, 2 with 20 etc and person 11 sits out the first pairing. After the first pairing, everyone moves one place to the left, Person 10 takes up Person 11's "sit out" position. Person 11 takes up Person 12's position.

| ODD NUMBER OF PARTICIPANTS - Everyone moves, one person is always "out" | | | | | | | | | | |
|---|---|---|---|---|---|---|---|---|---|---|
| 1 | 2 | 3 | 4 | 5 | 6 | 7 | 8 | 9 | 10 | |
| | | | | | | | | | | 11 |
| 21 | 20 | 19 | 18 | 17 | 16 | 15 | 14 | 13 | 12 | |

**Props, Aids, Special Forms**

Apart from the tables and chairs in the room, the only props needed for this event are a bell or whistle (to signal the time to move) and a timepiece. If one pair are slow to move on, then everyone else gets held up, so it is often necessary to "encourage" folks to move.

**Takeaways**

Delegates could be a little shell-shocked after Speed Networking. But they will have exchanged details with a large number of other networkers and they will have given themselves a lot of following-up to do. Because of the sheer frequency of movement, the adrenaline flows and most networkers say that they get a real "buzz" from these sessions.

## ALTERNATIVE NAMES

Any group can run the events presented above – and they can use whatever names they like for the various formats. None of the format names I used has been trademarked, but I would recommend that any groups try to stamp their own identity by using their own titles. Below, I have listed the various format names I used at Positive Networking meetings, then the names used by The Business Club where appropriate, and finally a few suggestions. Catchy names work well – but I recommend that you avoid suggestive or crude titles.

**Acid Test**

(The Business Club = Why Don't You Buy from Me?)

Suggestions

*Are You Credible?*

*Can You Recommend Me?*

**Ask Our Geeks**

Inspiration+ Clive Catton

Suggestions

*Networking Nerds*

*Simplifying The Technospeak*

**Boundarylessness**

Inspiration – Jack Welch (General Electric)

Suggestions

*You Scratch My Back ...*

*Removing The Silos*

**Bring A Prop**

(Inspiration – Andy Wilson

Suggestions

*Get Noticed And Be Memorable*

*Difficult To Forget*

**Deck Of Cards**

Inspiration – Max Boyce

Suggestions

*Jokers Wild*

*Networking Full House*

*A Fair Deal*

**Flipchart Fiesta**

Inspiration – Geoff Ramm

Suggestions

*I Buy And I Sell*

*Charts Of Opportunity*

**Getting To Know You**

(The Business Club = Knowing Me, Knowing You)

Suggestions

*12121*

*Mutual Help*

**Hammering Out A Deal**

Inspirations – Graham Child, Simon Hazeldine

Suggestions

*Effective Negotiation*

*Give And Take*

*Win Win*

**Knowledge Carousel**

Inspiration – Total Networking (Grantham)

Suggestions

*Magic Roundabout*

*What Goes Around, Comes Around*

**Matrix Networking**

(The Business Club = Speed Networking)

Suggestions

*Networking Table Shuffle*

*Networking Extravaganza*

**Mini Boardroom**

(The Business Club = Expanding Your Horizons)

Suggestions

*Think Tank*

*Brains Trust*

*Business Academy*

**Monopoly Of Wisdom**

Inspiration – Huntingdonshire Business Network

Suggestions

*Wealth Of Experience*

*What Do You Know?*

*All The Answers*

**Networking Bingo**

Inspiration – Craig Bunday

Suggestions

*Eyes Down*

*Full House*

**Networking Safari**

Suggestions

*Route March*

*The Great Trek*

*Networking Adventure*

**Open And Closed**

Suggestions

*Effective Questioning*

*Two Types of Question*

**Pair And Share**

Suggestions

*It Takes Two*

*Networking Twosome*

**Send Three And Fourpence**

Suggestions

*Chinese Whispers*

*Pass It On*

**Spanish Inquisition**

Suggestions

*Interrogation And Torture*

*Under The Spotlight*

**Speaker Event**

Suggestions

*Use "catchy" title, based on speaker's subject*

**Speed Networking**

Inspiration – many different groups

Suggestions

*Fast Networking*

*Networking Sprint*

# PART 9

# CLOSING ADVICE

“Brevity is the soul of wit.” (William Shakespeare)

“A good listener is not only popular everywhere, but after a while he gets to know something.” (Wilson Mizner)

At the beginning of this book, I explained how effective networking had enabled me to climb the corporate ladder, building a successful and enjoyable career for myself. By regularly demonstrating my abilities and achievements to others, I was able to be in the right place at the right time when opportunities arose.

More importantly, networking then enabled me to start from scratch and build a second career for myself as an SME. When starting my new business at the beginning of 2004, no-one on the SME circuit knew about (nor cared for) my large company experience. Through networking, I was able to establish a new reputation for myself and eventually "make it" a second time.

My advice to all people starting a business is to seriously look at incorporating networking into your marketing strategy – initially to become established and later to drive growth. When I left corporate life, I knew very little about the world of SMEs – but I had to learn very quickly. Regular attendance at networking events was crucial to me as I got to understand the challenges faced by small business owners. Undoubtedly networking made me a better adviser and a better business owner.

Networking can be hard work, especially when it involves early mornings and late nights. But it can be a really effective way of meeting customers, suppliers, collaborators, advisers and friends. You need to plan your activity, network regularly and do it well. ***Don't forget the Five Ps!***

I have covered a lot of different networking formats in this book and I have explained the various forms and props needed for each event. Additionally, for all your networking events, I strongly recommend that you issue a ***Delegate List***, complete with contact details for every person attending. Of course you must conform to relevant Data Protection rules and seek permission from the delegates – but issuing such a list will be appreciated by all concerned. If you can highlight new members or guests, that will enable your regulars to make early contact with the new faces. I suggest a Delegate List along the following lines:-

LOGO DELEGATE LIST "TITLE OF THE MEETING" DATE

| | Business Name | Delegate Name | Telephone | E-Mail Address | Nature of Business |
|---|---|---|---|---|---|
| 1 | | | | | |
| 2 | | | | | |
| 3 | | | | | |
| 4 | | | | | |
| 5 | | | | | |
| 6 | | | | | |
| 7 | | | | | |
| 8 | | | | | |
| 9 | | | | | |
| 10 | | | | | |
| 11 | | | | | |
| 12 | | | | | |
| 13 | | | | | |
| 14 | | | | | |
| 15 | | | | | |
| 16 | | | | | |
| 17 | | | | | |
| 18 | | | | | |
| 19 | | | | | |
| 20 | | | | | |
| 21 | | | | | |
| 22 | | | | | |
| 23 | | | | | |
| 24 | | | | | |
| 25 | | | | | |

So, include the following :-
Logo, "Delegate List", Title of the Event, Date, Sponsor's Logo, Number (for ease of identification), Business Name, Delegate Name, Telephone Number, E-mail Address, Nature of Business.

Milton Keynes UK
Ingram Content Group UK Ltd.
UKHW020816041123
431884UK00010B/271